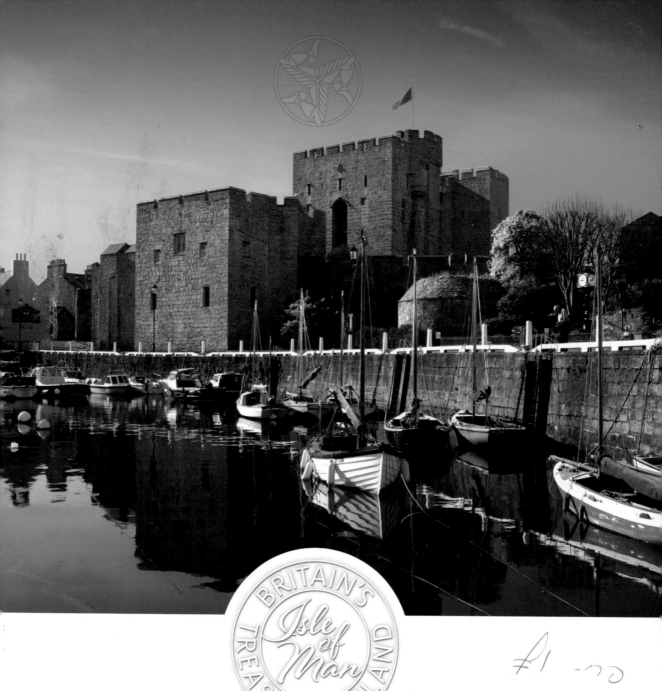

BRITAIN'S TREASURED ISLAND
Isle of Man

MILES COWSILL

D1493740

Lily
Publications

Published by:
Lily Publications, PO Box 33, Ramsey, Isle of Man IM99 4LP
Tel: +44 (0) 1624 898446   Fax: +44 (0) 1624 898449
E-mail: info@lilypublications.co.uk   Website: www.lilypublications.co.uk

Preface

Visitors to the Isle of Man may be surprised to learn that the Island is not part of the United Kingdom, Great Britain or the European Union. You won't need a passport if visiting the Island from the UK, however, the Island is a Crown dependency and part of the British Isles and the Commonwealth of Nations.

Upon arrival, you soon notice that you are somewhere rather different. The Isle of Man has its own government, laws, language, history, traditions, culture, gourmet specialities, folklore and fairy tales, and its own unique ecology. The island also issues its own stamps and coins. The Isle of Man lies in the Irish Sea between England, Scotland, Ireland and Wales and is 33 miles long and 13 miles wide, covers an area of 227 square miles and has a coastline of around a hundred miles. Nowhere on the Island is more than six and a half miles from the sea. Forty per cent of the Island is uninhabited, which means that this is a place where you can really get away from it all and go for miles without seeing anyone else. The island is a land of gently sloping beaches, rocky coves, sheer cliffs, valleys, thickly wooded glens, rolling hills and mountains with a castle or two thrown in for good measure.

This book gives, I hope, the reader an insight into *Britain's Treasured Island*, which continues to fascinate me, and I know many others. I consider myself very privileged to live on the Isle of Man, a truly unique and wonderful place.

I am grateful to all concerned who have assisted me with this publication, especially Sara Donaldson my fellow co-author and editor, Charles Guard (Culture Vannin), Vicky Harrop/Manx Museum and Patrica Tutt.

Miles Cowsill
May 2014

Right:
Ballacoshahan
Glade

Contents

Lily
Publications

Produced and designed by Lily Publications Ltd
PO Box 33, Ramsey, Isle of Man, British Isles, IM99 4LP
Tel: +44 (0) 1624 898446   Fax: +44 (0) 1624 898449
www.lilypublications.co.uk   E-Mail: info@lilypublications.co.uk
Printed and bound by Printo Trento, Italy © Lily Publications 2014

Introduction

PAST, PRESENT AND FUTURE

Below: Port Erin

Opposite: Ceiling in the Frank Matcham Gaiety Theatre in Douglas

Anyone seeking to prove the plausibility of time travel need surely look no further than the Isle of Man – a site of human occupation for around 9,000 years.

The landscape, history and culture of this independent island nation provide abundant evidence of those who at one time or another have made it their temporary or permanent home.

What is known about those who in turn have imposed or influenced governance here – namely Norsemen, the Irish, the Scots and the English – belongs to the much more recent period spanning the last 1,000 years. The Manx parliament, Tynwald, dates from the beginning of this time and stands (or rather, sits) as the longest-serving continuous parliament in the world.

Today the self-governing Isle of Man is switched on to telling the story of its long and often traumatic history whilst pointing simultaneously to a healthy economic present and very ambitious future. In 2013 the Island's economy achieved its 29th successive year of growth and, in terms of gross national income per head of population, was rated by the World Bank in the top 10 of 214 international economies.

The Island's airport, Ronaldsway, is served by the latest in high-capacity short-haul aircraft to achieve the twin goals of catering

Millennium Oakwood

for ever-increasing passenger traffic yet reducing the number of flights. The site is also home to the cutting-edge Science & Technology Park. But Ronaldsway has its place in ancient history too.

In 1943, during work on the airport, excavations revealed a spectacular treasure – an oblong dwelling house, along with tools, pottery and other artefacts, all believed to date from the second millennium of the Neolithic period (4,000 BC to 2,000 BC) and pointing to the importance of the Island's location on the earliest trade and migration sea routes. Further excavations in 2008 revealed Bronze Age artefacts and an exciting Mesolithic dwelling 3,000 years older than Stonehenge.

As the old and new mix within this perfect jewel of an island, we see a nation respectful of its natural habitat, proud of its heritage and yet with its feet very firmly in the 21st century. Innovation and a forward thinking attitude in business ensures that the Island stays attractive to international trade, as it has done throughout its history, while its relaxed atmosphere enhances the experience of its many visitors.

The Isle of Man is an island of contradictions – a leisurely pace of life mingles with exciting festivals while historic tradition links with modern life. With its unique past and its confident standing in today's world the Isle of Man is assured of an exciting future.

Left to right: TT at Bradden Bridge, Laxey Wheel. Douglas Marine and Mull Circle, Port Erin.

Place in the World

SO WHERE DOES THE ISLE OF MAN STAND?

Geographically, the Isle of Man is at the heart of the British Isles in the Irish Sea. On a clear day the 360° views from the highest point, Snaefell (Norse for 'snow mountain'), show you the neighbouring coastlines of Ireland, Scotland, England and Wales.

Myth, legend and folklore are all part of the rich fabric of Manx character and culture. The story goes that the Island was unintentionally created by Irish hero Finn McCool. In pursuit of a Scottish giant who tried to escape by swimming across the sea, Finn scooped up a huge mass of earth and hurled it with such force that it went over the giant's head, landed in the Irish Sea and became the Isle of Man. The hole he gauged out produced Northern Ireland's Lough Neagh.

In the real world, the Isle of Man's status constitutionally and administratively dates back to 1765 and is that of a self-governing British Crown dependency. Neither a part of the United Kingdom, nor part of the European Union, its inhabitants are however British citizens. The Island has its own parliament, flag, coat of arms, laws, taxation system, Manx language (though English is the everyday tongue), traditions, postage stamps and sterling-based currency. Responsibility for the Isle of Man's defence and foreign relations lies with the UK, with the Island paying an annual contribution in recognition of this agreement, which includes worldwide consular services for the Island's population.

The legal system of the Isle of Man is based upon the principles of English common law, however laws passed in Britain are not automatically passed on the Island. Indeed the Island has developed its own system which best serves the Manx population, most famously in relation to tax and company law.

THE CROWN DEPENDENCIES

The Isle of Man is one of three UK Crown dependencies along with the Channel Islands' Bailiwick of Jersey and Bailiwick of Guernsey. As each is self-governing it is not represented in the UK parliament.

Thus the Isle of Man appoints its own legislative assemblies through elections, and operates its own administrative, fiscal and legal systems and law courts. In relation to the European Union it has a unique status. Although neither a member nor associate member, the Island benefits from a special protocol which allows free movement of manufactured goods and agricultural products between the EU and the Isle of Man.

Head of State in each Crown dependency is Her Majesty Queen Elizabeth II, represented on each of the islands by a respective Lieutenant Governor. On the Isle of Man the Queen's title is Lord of Man and on the Channel Islands is Duke of Normandy.

Although each Crown dependency is self-governing, the Crown, acting through the Privy Council, is the ultimate authority, with a Privy Councillor for the Island having prime responsibility for the Island's affairs. The Privy Councillor is currently the Lord Chancellor and Secretary of State for Justice.

Internationally Dependencies are not seen as sovereign states in their own right, but are

Opposite page:
The Isle of Man is situated in the centre of the Irish Sea and on most days England, Ireland, Scotland and Wales can be seen from the upland areas of the Island.

Above: Tynwald Chambers in Douglas

seen as territories of the United Kingdom, however there is a framework set in place with the UK government to further develop their international identities.

TALKING OF THE MANX LANGUAGE...

Having survived the Island's long period of Norse rule, and despite in recent years being erroneously classified 'extinct' by the United Nations, the Manx Gaelic language is alive and well in the 21st century and, with strong support from the Manx Heritage Foundation, enjoying a healthy revival.

Manx-language playgroups, classes and degree courses cater for all ages, and the Island's 2014 Year of Culture celebrations embraced the opportunity to launch a national learn-at-home initiative. The language is one of the six Celtic languages alongside Irish, Scots Gaelic, Welsh, Cornish and Breton.

It was calculated that by mastering 20 given Manx Gaelic words each week (1,000 over the year), those participating could acquire a good basic understanding of how to converse in the traditional tongue, beginning with simple everyday phrases such as moghrey mie (good morning), fastyr mie (good afternoon) and oie vie (goodnight).

Concern for the survival of Manx Gaelic was evident in 1899 with the formation of the Manx

Language Society (Yn Cheshaght Ghailckagh), however as early as the 1800s there was worry over the failing language.

The Manx tongue had started a major decline by the start of the 20th century, due to outside influences on the Island, and by 1946 it was found that there were as few as 20 native speakers left. However, thanks to a group of dedicated activists in the 1930s, recordings were made of native speakers and the language was studied with the aim to preserve and promote its use. Ned Maddrell, the last recognised native speaker of Manx Gaelic died in 1974.

Manx culture, and the relationship between the Isle of Man and the other Celtic countries,

celebrated every year in the Yn Chruinnaght Manx and Inter-Celtic Festival, one of the Island's major events.

Most recently in the revival of the language, a young Port Erin singer, Ruth Keggin, has recorded an album of traditional and contemporary folk song arrangements in Manx Gaelic.

With around 1,700 Manx language speakers on the Island (as of the 2001 census statistics), and with the Year of Culture actively engaging those willing to learn their native language, the UNESCO classification was premature, with reports of the language's death greatly exaggerated.

In Manx, Isle of Man is Ellan Vannin.

From left to right: The Governor's official residence, Manx road sign, Manx notes and coins and Manx police with their white helmets at Tynwald Day.

Above: The Tynwald ceremony on Tynwald Hill is held in the morning in early July. The distinctive Manx flag is proudly flown from all government buildings on the Island and from a lot of residents' homes.

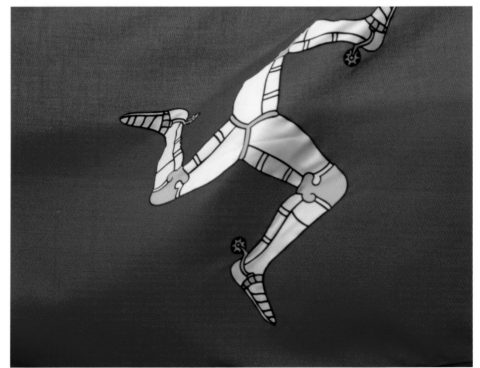

THE THREE LEGS OF MAN

If there is one thing above all others that most people immediately associate with the Isle of Man it is likely to be the three legs symbol. Sanctioned for use on the national flag in 1932, it became the centrepiece of a new Isle of Man Coat of Arms granted by Royal Warrant in 1996.

Today the symbol can be seen in many places across the Island, although its form is not always consistent. The most original and thought-provoking example is that created by Manxman Bryan Kneale for the 1979 Tynwald Millennium. His three-dimensional bronze sculpture at Ronaldsway's airport terminal stands 12 feet high.

Where, when and how the three legs and its use originated is not known for certain, but Manx legend has its own colourful explanation. The Island's king and protector is Manannan, the Celtic equivalent of Neptune, and he has two secret weapons: the ability to conjure up at will an impenetrable cloak of mist to hide the Island from prying eyes, and the magic to transform into the three legs and spin like a wheel to defeat would-be invaders.

Tracing the Island's earliest known use of the symbol in which the legs are clad in plate armour points you to Maughold and a carved stone cross, circa 14th century. The three legs also feature on the Manx Sword of State which, according to latest research, dates from the 15th century rather than earlier as previously believed.

Known as a triskele or triskelion, the three legs emblem probably originated as a sun symbol and has been used on the island of Sicily since the end of the seventh century BC. From the sixth century BC onwards it was also found on Greek coins. More significant to Isle of Man history is that the three legs featured on a silver penny dating from the 10th century and issued by the Norse king Anlaf Cuaran, who at some time in this period was a likely ruler of the Isle of Man. There is also evidence that the symbol was associated with 13th-century kings of Mann.

In 2013 the three legs ran to further fame when the emblem became the theme for the annual stamp issue of Isle of Man Post. The Island has administered its own postal service since 1973 and Manx stamp issues, often commemorating historic events and

Above: Scences from the annual Tynwald Day

Weather snaps

Generally, the Isle of Man experiences the driest months in April, May and June; the sunniest in May, June and July; and the warmest in July and August.

The highest known monthly sunshine total at Ronaldsway weather centre was 327 hours in July 1955. The highest temperature recorded here is 28.9°C (84°F).

Snaefell, the Island's highest point, is also the wettest as it receives the most annual rainfall, with an average of 1800mm around Snaefell compared to 900mm around the coast.

The coldest month is generally February with an average temperature of around 3°C. The lowest recorded temperature on the Isle of Man was -11.7 °C (10.9°F) recorded at Douglas in February 1895.

Right: Yn Chruinnaght at Ramsey

Opposite page: Derby Square, Douglas

outstanding achievement, are treasured by philatelists worldwide. Postage on all outgoing mail is valid only if Manx stamps are used.

'WHICHEVER WAY YOU THROW ME I WILL STAND'

This sentiment is a corruption of the legend inscribed on the Isle of Man's coat of arms: Quocunque Jeceris Stabit translates as 'wherever you throw it, it will stand'.

Interpreted as a statement of Manx character and resilience, it was put to the test in late March 2013. The livelihoods of many of the Island's livestock hill farmers were dealt a severe blow as a rare and extreme weather event struck the Isle of Man with very little warning, wreaking havoc within hours – and just a week before the calendar start of British Summer Time.

A colossal three-day snowfall, compounded by gale-force easterly winds gusting at up to 60 miles an hour, made many roads impassable, cut off small isolated communities in the west and north, brought down power and telephone lines, and buried flocks of grazing hill sheep under snow drifts up to 16 feet deep.

News of the event travelled fast, far and wide, well beyond the confines of the British Isles, but with the Island's communications crippled it was Facebook which helped alert local communities to the predicament of those farmers, people and places worst affected. An army of volunteers – men, women and children – rallied to the cause as the Island's overstretched emergency and public services worked around the clock in appalling conditions to restore supplies and order.

This rare event was completely at odds with Isle of Man's temperate climate of pleasant summers and mild winters.

Taking the motto in line with the Isle of Man's emblem, it is said to stand for not only the fortitude of the Island's people but also their position in the world, between the three kingdoms of Ireland, Scotland and England, as well as the stability of the actual symbol itself. Its earliest use on the Island dates back to around 1300, when the Island passed briefly to the Scottish Crown, with the motto also being that of the MacLeods of Lewis, however the motto first appeared on the Islands coinage in the 1660s.

SIZING UP THE ISLAND

At its extremities the Isle of Man is approximately 32 miles (52 km) long, 14 miles (22 km) wide and has a land area of 221 square

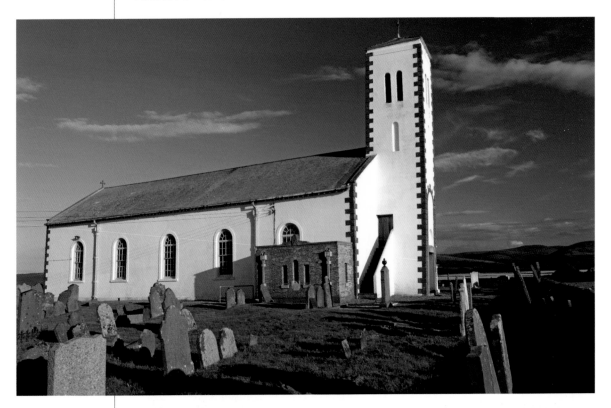

Above: Jurby
Church

Right: The Old
Grammar School
at Castletown

miles (572 sq km), of which more than 40% is uninhabited. There are more than 500 miles of roads and nowhere on the Island is further than 7 miles from the sea.

The last census, conducted in 2011, recorded a population of 84,497, an increase of 5.5% since the 2006 census. More than 50% of the population live in the capital, Douglas, and its immediate surrounds. The other major centres are the towns of Ramsey, Peel, Port Erin, Port St Mary and Castletown, the latter the Island's capital until the 1860s.

THE FINAL FRONTIER

The ultimate personal experience in Isle of Man time travel lies not in the landscape but in the stars. The Island has 26 accredited Dark Sky Discovery Sites – the largest concentration of such sites in Britain and so called because cloudless skies are frequent, greatly enhanced by low levels of light pollution. Even with the naked eye it is possible to see objects which are helping science to throw ever more light on the birth of the universe itself, 13.75 billion years ago.

The original seven Dark Skies locations, granted in October 2012 are the Axnfell plantation (near Laxey), Fort Island (near Castletown), Niarbyl (west coast), Port Soderick Brooghs (near Douglas), Smeale (north), the Sound (south coast) and Tholt y Will reservoir (central). A further 19 sites were added to these in January 2014: Ballaugh Beach, Ballanette Country Park, Ballure Reservoir, Clypse Kerrowdhoo, Conrhenny Car Park, Cregneash, Glen Mooar Beach, Glen Wyllin, Mooragh Promenade, Mount Murray, Peel Castle, Port Lewaigue Car Park, Port Soderick Car Park, Poulsom Park, Rushen Abbey, Sulby Reservoir Car Park, The Sloc, Tynwald Mills Car Park, West Baldwin Reservoir.

It is thought that due to light pollution 85% of the population have never seen a truly dark sky, but with a unique location, open landscape and small population the Isle of Man is perfectly suited to star-gazing. On a clear night, you can clearly see the Orion Nebula, the Milky Way and the Great Andromeda Galaxy with the

Stepping into history

The first time that a reigning British monarch set foot on the Isle of Man was on 24th August 1902, when King Edward VII and Queen Alexandra arrived in Douglas Bay on the Royal Yacht Victoria and Albert.

More than 50 years earlier, on 20th September 1847, Albert (Prince Consort husband of Queen Victoria) visited Ramsey and walked to the top of the hill known as Lhergy Frissel – an occasion celebrated and commemorated by the subsequent construction of the Albert Tower, a landmark which enjoys spectacular views over Ramsey Bay. Queen Victoria did not make shore on that historic day, remaining aboard the Royal Yacht.

July 1945 saw the first visit by King George VI and Queen Elizabeth (later the Queen Mother) to the Isle of Man. They were accompanied on the Island by Vice-Admiral William Spencer Leveson-Gower, the fourth Earl Granville, the Island's Governor, and his wife, the Queen's elder sister. During their stay the monarch was the first British Sovereign ever to preside over the ancient ceremony of the Manx government, Tynwald, at St John's.

naked eye. With binoculars or a telescope the skies become more spectacular – just remember to wrap up warm and make yourself comfortable for the night.

Visiting the Island around February to March, or September to October, you may also be lucky enough to glimpse the Aurora Borealis, commonly known as the Northern Lights. One of the few places in the British Isles to see the phenomenon, the crystal clear skies above the Island allow the observer to view the dancing hues that capture the imagination and leave a lasting impression of these magnetic storms.

THE GOOD LIFE

As well as consistently being one of Europe's most successful economies in tandem with the benefits of low taxation, low unemployment and high national income per head, the Isle of Man also gives residents plenty of fresh air, breathing space and a safe living environment.

Measured in terms of people per square mile (roughly 336 people per sq. mile), the population density is much lower than in either

and tourism being the main employers, and with a move towards technological industries spearheading the economy through the 21st century.

Education and healthcare are seen as being superior to the UK, with no long waiting lists, and while 'rush hour' is starting to creep into the Island's main towns, the pace of life is nowhere near as hectic as in the UK.

With a proud national heritage, the Island has a 'can-do' approach, embracing balance and a more relaxed approach to life. Being self-

Below: An exterior view of the Manx parliament building in Douglas, known locally as the 'Wedding Cake'

Opposite Page: *The House of Manannan*

Jersey or Malta. On the other hand, respect for the law and the local constabulary is high – as reflected by the Isle of Man's low crime rate.

Despite the worldwide recession, and the decline in the traditional industries of agriculture and fishing, the Island has reinvented itself as an international trade centre with offshore banking, manufacturing

governing the Island's government has the advantages of being able to tailor its actions to the needs of the people, and with a diverse mix of native Islanders and 'comeovers' the Island guarantees a vibrant community spirit.

With beautiful scenery, excellence in business and a 'freedom to flourish' attitude, the Isle of Man is all about the good life.

19

2 History

STORIES IN SHORT: THE PREHISTORIC AGES OF MAN

First inhabitants. People arrived on the Isle of Man about 9,000 years ago, a time when migrants from Europe were moving north and west to colonise the British Isles. Flint tools or weapons discovered at Glen Wyllin, near Kirk Michael, provide the earliest evidence of their presence.

Mesolithic Man. It is thought that in the period 7,000 BC to 4,000 BC the island's people were mainly hunter-gatherers – constantly on the move, taking their food from the land and sea. More than 80 early Mesolithic sites, mostly near the coast, have been identified and there are many more dating from the later Mesolithic period.

Neolithic Man. Discoveries from this period (4,000 BC to 2,000 BC) include pottery, stone axes, and monuments made from wood and stone, suggesting permanent settlements supported by farming rather than a nomadic lifestyle. This period also gave rise to large stone 'megaliths' – monuments such as the Meayll circle of burial chambers, unique in the British Isles for its layout. The most impressive megalith is Cashtal Yn Ard, though house building in the 19th century robbed it of many of its stones. Both monuments are in spectacular elevated coastal locations.

Bronze Age Man. Covering the period c. 2000 BC to 500 BC, this age is described in terms of Early, Middle and Late. Copper instead of stone and flint was used in making implements and weapons, as was gold. Much of the copper came from Bradda Head at Port Erin. The growth in farming and family settlements saw much of the island's earlier woodland cut down. About 400 burial sites have been identified – individual graves containing either a stone 'coffin' or cremation urn and covered with stones or earth.

Iron Age Man. Archaeologically speaking, in the British Isles this relates to the period 700 BC to around 500 AD – an age in which forts were built on hills and promontories to protect the communities within. More than 20 have been identified on the Isle of Man, notably the hill fort at South Barrule. This is the time of the Celts.

A LIGHTNING TOUR THROUGH HISTORY

Over the centuries the island's history has been shaped by the Irish Celts, who introduced Christianity, the Vikings, the Scots and the English.

The Celts brought their culture, language, magic and religion. Although the Isle of Man was rich in tin, a valuable commodity, the Roman Invasion largely bypassed the area, but we do know that Caesar knew of the tiny island in the Irish Sea, calling it 'Mona'. Around 500 AD Christianity arrived, and with it were built the keeills (tiny chapels), around 170 of these buildings litter the landscape. Celtic stone crosses were also carved, magnificent examples of which can be seen around the Island.

Norse settlers first arrived on the Isle of Man in around 800 AD. For 450 years the island was ruled by the Scandinavian Kings of

Above: Between the high ground of North Barrule and the coast at Port Cornaa lies the Neolithic burial chamber of Cashtal Yn Ard

Left: Manx crosses at Maughold church

Mann and the Isles, the isles being the 'Sodorenses' or southern islands, far to the north of Man and including Islay, Lewis, Mull and Skye. Administration of the Island led to a Manx parliament meeting at Tynwald Hill in St John's around 900 AD, and has been the Island's governing power ever since. During

escaped to the Isle of Man and was received with honour by King Godred, his cousin. The king died in 1070 and was succeeded by his son Fingal, but in 1079, after two failed attempts, Godred Crovan took control of the Island. He famously spared the Islanders, but not before allowing his men to plunder the

Below: Peel Castle

Opposite page:
*Monks Bridge,
Ballasalla*

this time the Island was also situated within Viking trade routes and may have been an important centre for commerce.

The power struggle to establish control of the Irish Sea area involved rivals such as Irish chieftains, the Earls of Orkney and the formidable kings of Scotland and Norway. The Isle of Man, with its unique placement, was, as a result, at the centre of these skirmishes, and an important asset.

The *Chronicles of Mann* gives us the names of the first kings of Man. Godred, son of Sytric is recorded as king in 1066. After the battle of Stamford Bridge a Norwegian, Godred Crovan,

Island before leaving. During his 16 year reign Crovan rebuilt the Island, and his descendants ruled Man until 1265. He became the King Orry of legend.

In 1266 the Isle of Man was ceded to the King of Scotland following successive attempts to claim the kingdom of the Isles. When Magnus, the last of Godred Crovan's descendants died without legitimate issue, Alexander, King of Scotland claimed the Island as his own. Ownership passed successively between Scotland and England over the next 150 years. During this time of change the Church grew, along with its power and influence.

23

Above: Harry Kelly's Cottage at Cregneash

Right: Nautical Museum at Castletown

Opposite page: Castle Rushen

From 1406 to 1736 the Lords of Mann were the Stanley family of Lancashire, the title subsequently passing to their kin, the Dukes of Atholl. Sir John Stanley was granted the Isle of Man, in perpetuity, as a reward for his loyalty to the Crown by Henry IV. Up until 1504, and the succession of Thomas Stanley, 2nd Earl Derby, the Stanley family held the rarely used title of King of Man, however Thomas reverted to the title Lord of Man, which was used thereafter. Despite a sustained line of Lords, the Isle of Man was not without dispute. Due to the Royalist activity of James Stanley, 7th Earl of Derby, the English Civil War visited the Island in 1651 leading to the famous rebellion of Illiam Dhone and his militia.

In 1765 the island was revested in the British Crown as a Crown dependency, following the death of James Murray, 2nd Duke of Atholl, and King George III became sovereign. Successive sovereigns since that date have been George IV (1820), William IV (1830), Victoria (1837), Edward VII (1901), George V (1910), Edward VIII (1936, abdicated), George VI (1936) and Elizabeth II (1952).

EARLY PROSPERITY

Treasures unearthed in the Manx landscape suggest that in the 10th and 11th centuries the island's rulers were themselves very enterprising traders. Discoveries have included hoards of coins and a large number of silver rings which were worn on the arm, the total of the latter almost equal to the number found in the whole of Ireland.

More than 400 coins, along with arm rings, silver and ornaments dating from around 970 were discovered at Ballaquayle in 1894. In 1972 coins which formed part of another hoard are believed to have been produced on the island at a mint established in about 1025. The Kirk Michael hoard, buried around 1065, contained English, Irish, Norman and Manx coins along with rings and other jewellery. The hoard is especially important as the coins found came from all over the world and point to the importance of the Island in Viking trade routes.

The Island is still revealing its treasures today. In 2003 a hoard found in Glenfaba

Digging into history

'For anyone digging into the past the Isle of Man is a veritable treasure trove. We found a long-lost church, the body of a 6th-century woman, and a stone slab covered in ancient writing. Not bad for three days' work!'

So said Tony Robinson, presenter of television's popular archaeology-based series Time Team, when the programme visited the Isle of Man during its 14th season. Their aim over the weekend was to excavate the site of a keeill (a small ancient chapel) which lay beneath the seventh fairway of the golf course at Mount Murray. During the three-day excavation in 2007 the Team were allowed to dig the only known keeill to remain undisturbed on the Island, as well as taste the Island's hospitality. Discovery of an ogham stone and a cross slab helped in the dating of the keeill, and allowed the Island's archaeologists a starting point for further research and examination.

yielded more than 460 silver coins and 25 ingots. As recently as 2013 another small hoard, containing silver ingots and a piece of a

Ill-gotten gains

Fortune hunters of the least popular kind were rife in the 1930s, the bustling summer crowds of Isle of Man holidaymakers providing easy pickings for unscrupulous pickpockets. One such criminal received his comeuppance when an intended victim happened to be a retired policeman.

Michal Vassilivith, alias Henry K. Ankel, a 36 year old Continental thief of 'considerable experience' decided to pick the pocket of a gentleman on the steamer at Douglas during the summer of 1933. Vassilivith had served prison sentences during the previous 12 years in Berlin, Vienna and Prague. He had been deported from England in 1930 and the authorities had no idea how he had managed to re-enter the country.

Unfortunately for the thief his victim just happened to be an ex-constable from Liverpool. He was sentenced to three months imprisonment under the Vagrancy Act.

silver brooch were found at Andreas, an ingot found nearby in 2009 were presumably part of the same group.

COINS TO TREASURE

Innovative postage stamps are not the only Isle of Man issue with which today's serious collectors concern themselves. For more than 25 years numismatics worldwide have taken a shine to coinage issued by the Manx Treasury.

Every coin features an effigy of the current Head of State and Lord of Mann, Her Majesty Queen Elizabeth II, sculpted by Ian Rank-Broadley. Manx coins are consistent prize winners, the 1990 Penny Black also being notable as the world's first pearl-black coin. Regular bestselling coin successes amongst collectors are those themed on the TT and Christmas.

The official currency on the Island is the Manx pound, which is not legal tender in the UK, however the UK pound is recognised as legal on the Isle of Man with an equivalent value to the Island's coinage.

The earliest 'modern' Manx coins found date from 1668, although unearthed hoards point towards a much earlier manufacture. Up until 1840 the Island had its own currency, however following a British Act of Parliament Manx coinage was replaced with its British counterpart, until the Island began producing its own currency following decimalisation in 1971 .

Banknotes were issued by the Island's banks from the 18th century onwards, but in 1961 Tynwald revoked existing licenses and charged the Isle of Man Bank with production its behalf. The first Isle of Man bank notes were issued in 1961 in denominations of ten shillings (50 pence today), one pound and five pounds.

AGATHA'S GOLDEN YARN

In 1930 one of the world's greatest

28

Another millennium celebration

On 9th March 2000 the island's primary school children planted 6,868 trees (one for each child) in just two hours to create the Millennium Oakwood at Bradda, close to the hospital. A day of celebrations involved the children being transported from every part of the Island, with professional entertainers greeting them at the site. Konnie Huq from children's television programme Blue Peter presided over the official opening, much to the delight of the assembled crowd.

At the wood's centre is a giant-sized replica of the Manx Sword of State and a sculpture representing the Solar System.

Island. Each box contained a token entitling the bearer to a reward of £100, with the boxes hidden in locations known only to her. Christie gave the clues to finding the boxes in a short story called *Manx Gold*, serialized in five installments in the *Daily Dispatch* newspaper in May of that year.

Adverts were also placed in National newspapers enticing the public to visit the Island:

'A thrilling mystery story by Mrs Agatha Christie, the famous novelist, reprinted from the "Daily Dispatch", together with full particulars to enable you to join in this novel Free Competition, may be obtained from N.C. Clague, Publicity Department, Isle of Man'

To keep up the momentum and promote the hunt further throughout the tourist season,

Right: Laxey Wheel

Opposite page: Cregneash

exponents of crime novels hatched a cunning plan to entice more tourists to the Isle of Man. Agatha Christie was commissioned by an Isle of Man tourism committee to write a short story, in which cryptic clues were given to the location of four gold snuff boxes buried on the

the story was re-published in a promotional booklet *June in Douglas* which was distributed around the Island.

Three of the snuff boxes were found; one at Fort Island, one on Peel Hill and one near the Druid's Circle above Port Erin.

3 | Towns & Villages

CASTLETOWN *(BALLEY CHASHTAL)*

This ancient capital of the Isle of Man sits at the south of the Island, sheltered by Castletown Bay with the Langness Peninsula to the east.

One of the oldest towns in Britain, dating from 1090, Castletown is also home to Castle Rushen, one of the finest preserved medieval castles in the British Isles and still in use today. During its long history the castle has been the home to the Kings and Lords of Mann, the seat of government, a mint, courts and a prison. The foundations of the castle date back to the times the last Norse Kings of Mann. Today you can visit the castle museum, run by Manx National Heritage, and take a closer look at the mighty fortress that once dominated the Island.

Once a thriving fishing town with narrow streets and pretty fisherman's cottages, commercial traffic in the town mostly ended in the 1970s, making Castletown a peaceful area, now more centred on finance and business. But if it's maritime history you are after, the Nautical Museum is the place to go. A fascinating discovery in 1935 unearthed an 18th century schooner, *Peggy*, walled up in her original boathouse, which now houses the museum. Possibly the worlds oldest yacht, she is recognised as being 'of extraordinary maritime importance', having lay undiscovered for 100 years after the death of her owner.

Of course, being the ancient capital the

Right: Castletown

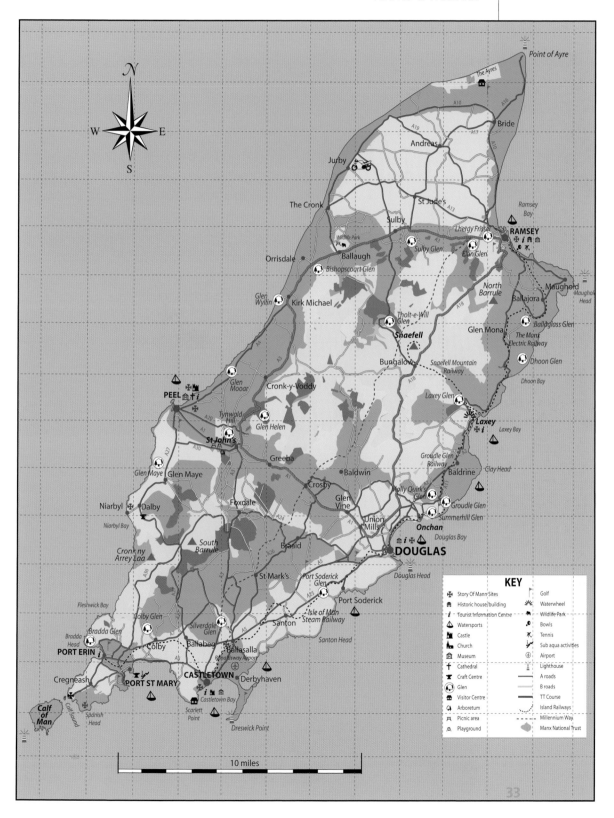

KEY

Story Of Mann Sites		Golf	
Historic house/building		Waterwheel	
Tourist Information Centre		Wildlife Park	
Watersports		Bowls	
Castle		Tennis	
Church		Sub aqua activities	
Museum		Airport	
Cathedral		Lighthouse	
Craft Centre		A roads	
Glen		B roads	
Visitor Centre		TT Course	
Arboretum		Island Railways	
Picnic area		Millennium Way	
Playground		Manx National Trust	

Above:
Castletown
Right: Douglas
commercial centre

town is home to some of the Island's most important buildings. The Old House of Keys was the meeting place for the Manx parliament from 1709 until 1869 when Douglas took over as the Island's capital, and is open to visitors, while the Old Grammar School dates from around 1200, when it was the town's original church, and now houses a reconstruction of the old school. A walk to the historic town square will allow you to see the monument to Cornelius Smelt, still in its unfinished state after Islanders refused to pay for a statue to grace the memorial. The clock presented to the Island by Queen Elizabeth I fared better, as despite only ever having one hand it continues to tell the time!

DOUGLAS *(DOOLISH)*

Nestled on the sheltered east coast, the town of Douglas is the capital of the Isle of Man. With a population of around 28,000 this is the largest town on the Island, home to its government and a centre for finance and business, as well as a popular tourist destination.

The town grew from a small fishing village into an important port in the late 17th century, thanks to its sheltered position and focus on trade. During the 18th century Douglas also became the focal point for the 'running trade'. Due to high taxes imposed in Britain on goods such as wine, brandy, tea, spices and tobacco, merchants imported their stock to the Isle of Man, then 'ran', or smuggled, the

From left to right: Horsetram. Villa Marina, Gaiety Theatre and Marina, North Quay.

Next page: Dougas Bay with Ben My-Chree arriving from Heysham.

35

Above: Marina at Douglas

Right: Laxey harbour and beach

consignments to men waiting on the British mainland. While this made Douglas wealthy, the British government soon grew weary and with Revestment in 1765 the running trade was hit hard. Despite this blow to the town's income, the town focused on legitimate trade and continued to prosper.

Georgian England was attracted by the low cost of living on the Island, with the upper classes arriving in Douglas and building their impressive town houses. The early Victorian tourist boom soon brought a different kind of prosperity to Douglas, as it became a popular destination for wealthy travellers. The introduction in 1830 of a regular Steam Packet service between Douglas and Liverpool, along with the rapid expansion of the railways, made visiting the Island easier and more attractive. It soon became a regular holiday spot for workers from the north of England.

By 1869 Douglas' expansion and wealth prompted a move by parliament to the seaside town, and it became the Island's capital.

With the tourist trade came hotels, boarding houses, theatres, ballrooms, parks and other entertainments to keep the visitors happy. The promenade and piers catered for those with expectations of a traditional seaside holiday. Douglas continued to be a popular destination well into the 20th century, only falling out of favour for a short time when the introduction of package holidays abroad enticed travellers to more exotic places. However, Douglas is again a popular haven for those wanting to enjoy a holiday with lots on offer, with daily sailings bring visitors from all over the world to the port.

Not one to rest on its laurels, the town is also known for the rapid growth of its business sector which has modernised the town in recent years, with a focus on finance, e-gaming, shipping and, something that may surprise visitors, its space industry. This new expansion has brought fashionable shops, restaurants and entertainment, which stand alongside more traditional attractions, such as such as the horse-drawn trams that continue to travel the promenade during the summer months.

LAXEY (LAKSAA)

Above: Pretty Laxey inner harbour

With a name derived from the old Norse for 'Salmon River', Laxey sits in a deep glen on the east coast of the Island between the towns of Douglas and Ramsey.

The small fishing village expanded in the late 18th century when mineral deposits were discovered and a thriving mining industry grew around the area. By the mid 19th century as many as 1,000 men were employed in the mine which produced the bulk of the British Isles' zinc and a substantial amount of lead ore, copper and silver.

Laxey is home to *Lady Isabella*, the largest working waterwheel in the world, known as the Great Laxey Wheel. Built to pump water out of the mines, which closed in 1929, she stands 75 feet tall, looking out over the valley. The Laxey Heritage Trail, a two-hour circular leisurely walk around the area starts at the waterwheel, providing a fascinating insight into this part of the Island's history.

Right: Summer in Peel

Below: The ruins of Peel Castle

Also to be found in Laxey are the Laxey Woollen Mills, the last working woollen mills on the Island and the Snaefell Mountain Railway, which will transport you to the top of the Isle of Man's highest point.

PEEL (PURT NY H-INSHEY)

Peel, on the west of the Island, situated at the mouth of the River Neb, is also known as the Isle of Man's only city. As seat of the Bishops of Sodor and Man, the town houses the current

Royal prisoners. Eleanor, Duchess of Gloucester, was imprisoned for 14 years until her death and held captive under the chancel of Peel's cathedral, accused of treason and sorcery against Henry VI. Second wife of Humphrey, Duke of Gloucester (1390–1447), her husband became heir to the throne in 1435 after the death of his brother John, Duke of Bedford. Consulting astrologers, who predicted that a life-threatening illness would overcome the king, rumours led to Eleanor's arrest in

Below: Looking north over Peel

Cathedral Church of St German, while the ancient cathedral of St Germans, now a ruin, can be found within the walls of Peel Castle.

Looking out towards Ireland, Peel is the perfect place to witness breathtaking sunsets which frame St Patrick's Isle, after which the town is named. Purt ny h-Inshey meaning Port of the Island. Now a relaxing haven on the west coast, the area has seen its fair share of excitement, from smugglers and invaders to

1441 and subsequent imprisonment. Her ghost is said to haunt the castle.

PORT ERIN (PURT CHIARN)

On the Mull peninsula, in the south of the island, sits the popular resort of Port Erin. The Manx name of Purt Chiarn translates as Lord's Port or Iron Port, hinting at its importance in times gone by. A haven for smugglers in the times of the 'running trade', the pretty village

Above: Looking towards Port Erin from Bradda Head

Opposite page: Milners Tower

expanded in the 1880s to become a favourite for Victorian holidaymakers from the UK.

Sheltered by Bradda Head to the north and Castle Rocks in the south, the bay is attractive for its calm water, ideal for watersports or family beach days. Looking out towards Ireland and the Mountains of Mourne, this is also the gateway to the Calf of Man nature reserve and bird observatory, with boat trips leaving from the harbour.

The Erin Arts centre is based here, as is the Port Erin Railway Museum, and for the sports enthusiast the Rowany golf course boasts a superb 18-hole course.

PORT ST MARY (PURT LE MOIRREY)

Across the neck of the Mull peninsula, just a short distance from Port Erin, lies the fishing village of Port St Mary, home to the famous Manx Queenie. A variety of small scallop, this delicacy is celebrated every year with the Queenie Festival when visitors and Islanders alike come to dedicate a weekend to the sea, fine food and the Isle of Man's marine heritage.

Another reason to visit the village, apart from its beautiful scenery and thriving port, is the 9-hole golf course designed by George Duncan, the 1920 British Open Champion. Winning the first Open to be played since 1914, he was the subject of one of the greatest comebacks in golf history, winning the Championship after overcoming a 13 stroke deficit in the final round to beat 1902 winner Sandy Herd by two strokes. The course he designed is a hilly course with spectacular views and the only 9-hole course on the Island.

RAMSEY (RHUMSAA)

The largest town in the north, and the second largest town in the Isle of Man, Ramsey was named by the Vikings as Wild Garlic River, possibly due to the abundance of the plant along the riverbanks.

Located closest to Scotland and England, and in a wide sweeping bay, the area has a long and turbulent history. As the landing place of many an invader Ramsey can be forgiven for its lack of ancient buildings. Mentioned in the

Above: Port St Mary

Right: Parliament Square, Ramsey

Chronicles of Mann, the town saw Godred Crovan (King Orry) land on his way to take claim to the Island in 1079 AD, then down the centuries as the Island witnessed many a power struggle the town saw numerous visitors, both friendly and hostile.

A more friendly visit to Ramsey occurred in 1847 when Queen Victoria and Prince Albert visited the Island. While the Queen decided to stay on-board the Royal Yacht, Albert went ashore, climbing a hill above town to admire the view. This is commemorated by the Albert Tower.

Modern day visitors can take advantage of Mooragh Park with its 40 acres of gardens and extensive boating lake, the Grove Museum of Victorian Life and Milntown house, the home of the Christian family, whose members include Illiam Dhone and Fletcher Christian, made famous for the mutiny on the Bounty.

ST. JOHN'S *(BALLEY KEEILL EOIN)*

Home to the ancient Tynwald, the Island's parliament, the small village of St John's plays host to Tynwald Day every July (usually around the 5th). Tynwald Hill has been the Isle of Man's assembly place since at least the time of the Vikings, when new laws and disputes were heard, pronouncements made and transactions settled.

This tradition still takes place, with thousands of people flocking to the village every year to hear the Island's laws from the past year read out. The reading takes the form of both English language and Manx declarations, read by the Deemsters in front of dignitaries and the gathered crowds. Presided over by the Lieutenant Governor of the Island, unless the Queen Elizabeth (the Lord of Man), or a member of the Royal family attends in her stead, this is the most important day in the Island's calendar.

Situated in the west of the Island, not far from Peel, the rest of the year sees St. John's as a pretty village, unassuming in its importance.

4 | Heritage

Opposite page:
Herring tower at
Langness

THE STORYTELLERS

The Manx certainly know how to tell a story. The Isle of Man is very well known for its folklore, tales and fairy tradition, but the narrative which to date has reached the widest audience has to be that told by Manx National Heritage.

Presented to wide acclaim for visitors and Islanders alike, the story of what defines Manx sense of place, culture and unique national identity spans 10,000 years of history and has many aspects.

Some stories are set in stone, such as ancient monuments in the form of decorated grave markers and memorial stones found in parishes across the Island. Prehistoric sites tell of Iron Age promontory forts, Neolithic graves and tombs and Mesolithic occupation. The Scandinavian influence is much in evidence in the form of Viking boat burials and Norse long houses. A surprising number of keeills (small earth and stone chapels) also dot the landscape.

As the Island's statutory heritage agency, Manx National Heritage is based at the Manx Museum in Douglas and is responsible for national museums, monuments, archives, art and more than 3,000 acres of landscape. The museum itself is dubbed the Island's treasure house and was extended to accommodate a new National Art Gallery, a Map Gallery and a Prehistoric Archaeology Gallery, the latter attracting a Museum of the Year Award as the best of its kind in the British Isles. The extension was officially opened by the Queen in 1989.

More recently a digital museum, called the imuseum, has been opened in Douglas. Housing a selection of the Island's archives, the repository allows visitors to start telling their own stories. Manx newspapers, parish records, images of the Island and its people are all gathered under one roof, and are also available digitally online, along with art collections, social history documents and a manuscript collection. The perfect place to start researching the Island's history, the building is a haven for family and social historians.

THE MAGIC OF MANANNAN

Winning awards is something of a habit for Manx National Heritage. Peel's interactive House of Manannan welcomed its first visitors in 1997 and received the accolade 'British Isles Museum of the Year' – not once but twice.

The state-of-the-art presentation brings to life the mythological sea god and shape-shifting protector of the Isle of Man, Manannan, who speaks from a lofty position at the top of Spooyt Vane (white spout), a dramatic waterfall on the edge of Glen Mooar south of Kirk Michael. Telling the unfolding story – of pagan Celts and Vikings and their conversion to Christianity, of the medieval Kingdom of Mann and the Isles, of maritime history, smuggling and fishing – is Egodonas, a Celt.

Integral to the story is St Patrick's Isle, where stands Peel Castle. The ruins encompassed by the castle's curtain wall include St Patrick's Church and the 13th-century Cathedral of St German. Manx Christianity was established here in the 6th century and stood its ground when pagan

Vikings came in the late 8th century. In the 11th century Peel Castle's status was elevated to that of the ruling seat of the Norse Kingdom of Man and the Isles.

In 1979, the year of the Tynwald Millennium, the enduring cultural connections between the Manx and the Scandinavians was further enhanced by the arrival on the Isle of Man of *Odin's Raven* – a replica Norse longship made in, and sailed from, Norway. This gift to the Manx nation is another of the treasures displayed in the House of Manannan.

A NEW CHAPTER IN THE PEGGY STORY

As remarkable stories go, that of *Peggy* is up there with the best – and it features two remarkable protagonists. One is *Peggy* herself, an armed yacht built in 1790 and unique today for a very impressive CV. This credits her as the oldest surviving Manx craft, the oldest example of a dropped keel vessel and the grandmother of all yachts. Her condition defies her great age and she also merits a Grade 1 listing on the National Historic Ships Register for her 'extraordinary' maritime importance.

The other character in the story is the man for whom *Peggy* was built – Manx banker, politician (a member of the House of Keys),

inventor, eccentric and suspected smuggler George Quayle (1751–1835). After his death the boat was of no interest to the Quayle family and she was put into the boathouse he had created for her, which was subsequently walled up with masonry.

It wasn't until 1935 that *Peggy* was rediscovered and later gifted to the Manx Museum by a family descendant. In the 1950s the property of which the boathouse was part, in Bridge Street, Castletown, became the Nautical Museum and *Peggy* has attracted many visitors in the decades since.

Today *Peggy* is the subject of a Manx National Heritage conservation project, the logistics of which are complex. Her basement boathouse alongside Castletown harbour is prone to flooding and, with predictions of exceptionally high tides in 2015, the need to remove her well in advance of this is crucial. So too is the need to avoid inflicting irreparable damage during the process, as access is difficult and her great age necessitates sympathetic handling. She is a wooden boat with metal fixings, some of which have corroded, and once relocated to a site easily accessible to public viewing it is thought that it will take at least three years to

Previous page:
Rushen Abbey,
Ballasalla

Opposite page:
Laxey Wheel

Above left:
Oddin's Raven at
Peel

Above right:
Manx Museum

The Great LAXEY WHEEL & Mines Trail

Above: Laxey Mines

dry out her timbers. The overall objective is to return *Peggy* to her Nautical Museum home with the guarantee of a further long lease of life to come.

VINTAGE ISLE OF MAN

Today, getting around the island on public transport is an eye-opening experience in time travel. Restored Victorian electric and steam railways, faithfully maintained in line with their original drawings and specifications, and representing a significant ongoing investment, take you north and south from Douglas to the terminus stations of Ramsey and Port Erin respectively.

The steam railway is officially known as the Isle of Man Railway, and was the first rail service to be opened on the Island in 1874. It is also the longest 3-foot narrow gauge steam railway in the British Isles. Operated by the Isle of Man government, the steam railway is popular with tourists, but is very much a working transport system, taking travellers along a scenic one hour route to Port Erin.

The Manx Electric Railway began its life 20 years after the steam railway made its mark

on the Island, but is still going strong today. Originally named the Douglas & Laxey Coast Electric Tramway, tram journeys began in 1893, with the company becoming the Isle of Man Tramways and Electric Power Co Ltd in 1894. Following expansion the route was taken over by the Manx Electric Railway Company Ltd in 1902. Travelling to and from Ramsey on the trams today you may even board one of the two oldest tramcars still in continuous operation in the world, car numbers one and two.

Horsepower is part of the story too. The horse-drawn trams, which from mid-May to mid-September trot up and down the two-mile length of Douglas Promenade, maintain a tradition that began in 1876 and survives today as the world's oldest tramway of its kind. All 21 carriages and the double-decker tram are originals. At the end of their working lives the horses enjoy all the comforts and pampering of a dedicated equine retirement home – a popular visitor attraction in itself.

If leisurely mountaineering is more your thing, why not board the only electric mountain railway in the British Isles? Operating

Above: Lady Evelyn, Laxey

Left: Manx Electric Railway (MER) at Cornaa

53

from 1895 the Snaefell Mountain Railway, departing from the village of Laxey, transports visitors up to the summit of Snaefell, the Islands highest peak. From there you can see all seven kingdoms on a clear day, England, Scotland, Wales, Ireland, Mann, Heaven and the Sea.

CARVED CROSSES

No mention of Isle of Man heritage is complete without acknowledgement of the exquisitely carved stone crosses that litter the Island. These monuments date back to the early introduction of Christianity to the Isle of Man and are of Celtic and Norse origin. Over 200 examples of these carved monuments have so far been found on the Island.

The earliest examples of these decorated stone slabs were found in Maughold parish and date from around 650 AD to the 8th century. It is thought that Maughold was the centre for a religious community during this period and was the site of a Celtic monastery in 600 AD. Although the monuments are predominantly Christian, the earliest examples are actually pre-Christian with Ogham script carvings covering the stone. Over 40 slabs can be seen at Kirk Maughold, the largest concentration of such examples on the Island,

ranging from simple carvings to intricate Celtic knot-work.

The crosses, however, are not all of Celtic origin. Spectacular Norse crosses can also be found in a number of parishes, dating up to the 13th century and mixing Christian imagery with pagan mythology. Two crosses are actually signed by the man who carved them, Gaut, son of Bjorn from Kolli, and can be seen in Andreas and Kirk Michael.

Philip Kermode, first Director of the Manx Museum, collected and numbered most of the known crosses, placing them for safekeeping either in the Manx Museum or in the churches of the parish in which each stone was found, and where they can still be found today. His book *Manx Crosses*, published in 1907, lists and fully describes the stones. Thanks to his foresight these monuments have been preserved and replicas of the collection can be found on display at the Manx Museum.

One of the most spectacular examples of carving found on the Island is the cross depicting the crucifixion found on the Calf of Man in 1773. Once privately owned it is now held in the Manx Museum. Intricately carved with a fully clothed figure of the crucified Christ, and a bearded spear bearer before him, this fragment dates to around 800 AD was probably part of an altar piece for the small chapel on the island. Anyone familiar with the *Book of Kells* and the *Lindisfarne Gospels* will recognise the artwork style.

KEEILLS AND CHURCHES

It is thought that Christianity came to the Isle of Man in the late 5th or early 6th century, carried by missionaries from Ireland. Although St Patrick had some relationship with the Island, with St Patrick's Isle and the parish churches of Kirk Patrick named after him, as well as the site of St Patrick's Chair, no one knows for sure if he actually set foot upon Manx soil. His legacy however is here for everyone to see.

Early medieval chapels, or keeills, have made their mark on the landscape. There are roughly 200 sites of keeills around the Isle of

Castletown station

55

Above: St
Trinians's

Man, although only around 35 are readily identifiable as such. Their origins are largely unknown, however it may be that a keeill was built in each treen, an ancient unit of land generally consisting of four farms or 'quarterlands', on the Island. Made of earth and stone, keeills may have been small chapels for family groups, monastic cells or areas of worship attached to burial grounds. Priest's houses have been found within a few keeill enclosures.

It is thought that the buildings date from the time of early Christian settlement, however recent research may place their construction to around the time of the Norse invasions. In 2007 Channel Four's *Time Team* excavated a keeill situated on the golf course at Mount Murray, the only known undisturbed example on the Island. During the weekend dig an ogham stone and a cross slab were found, which may help further in dating the chapels.

More structured churches were built following the ecclesiastical change to a system of parishes around the 13th century. A few church buildings on the Island still bear evidence of these early constructions, for example the roofless, medieval chapel of St Trinian's in Marown. The Old Grammar School in Castletown is a fine example of how churches on the Island have accommodated change, being turned from a place of worship to a place of learning in the early 1700s.

Today there are many fine examples of sacred architecture on the Isle of Man, from the ancient established Church, to Methodist chapels such as the first Wesleyan meeting place on the Island, Peel Chapel.

Government

A THOUSAND YEARS IN A DAY

'Our little nation is the only Norse nation now on earth that can shake hands with the days of the Sagas and the Sea-Kings. Then let him who will laugh at our primitive ceremonial. It is the badge of our ancient liberty, and we need not envy the man who can look on it unmoved.'

Hall Caine *(from The Little Manx Nation)*

Burial sites and traces of Norse-style homesteads suggest that Vikings settled on the Isle of Man and intermarried with the local population from around the late 8th century onwards.

With them came their custom of holding an annual open-air summer gathering of all free men to announce new laws, do business and settle disagreements. In Norse this occasion was known as 'Thingvollr', from which the word Tynwald was derived. More than a thousand years later the tradition continues on the Isle of Man in the form of Tynwald Day, a midsummer event treasured by the Manx as testimony to their heritage and independence and by the proud fact that Tynwald functions today as the oldest continuous parliament in the world.

The setting for this big occasion and national holiday, usually on 5th July, is ceremonial Tynwald Hill, an artificial four-tiered circular mound in the village of St John's. Covered with turf and one of the Isle of Man's most distinctive landmarks, it is said to be made of stones bonded with soil from each of the island's 17 ancient parishes. Although the hill's origin is generally ascribed to the

13th century, there is strong conviction amongst historians that the site's significance as a meeting place could date back as early as the Bronze Age (c. 2000 to 500 BC).

Records of Tynwald Day suggest that over the centuries the proceedings have remained virtually unchanged. The ceremony is presided over by a representative of the British monarchy, usually the island's resident Lieutenant-Governor but on occasion by a member of the Royal Family. The first British sovereign to do so, as Lord of Mann, was King George VI in 1945. In 1979, the year assigned as the Tynwald Millennium (although there is no precise historical evidence to validate this), the honour fell to his daughter and heir Her Majesty Queen Elizabeth II, the current Lord of Mann.

For the many spectators attending the event, the day's main business begins as the bearer of the ancient Manx Sword of State leads the dignitaries from the Royal Chapel of St John's along the Processional Way to their respective places on Tynwald Hill. The reading, first in English and then in Manx, of new laws introduced in the parliamentary year is followed by the open invitation to anyone present wishing to present a Petition for Redress to do so – a procedure which is all part and parcel of the island's time-honoured democratic process.

When the further formalities and pageantry are finally concluded, the mood gives way to the fun and festivities of the Tynwald Fair's market, music and dancing. Displayed in the Royal Chapel is a Tynwald exhibition and also

The Old House of Keys

For anyone with an interest in politics, and in particular the Manx political system and history, the restored Old House of Keys in Castletown is a must-visit attraction. Not only does it give a fascinating insight into how life in the debating chamber used to be but also invites public participation in morning and afternoon sessions.

In Tynwald Court, all 35 elected members of parliament sit together to deal with finance, policy and secondary legislation, presided over by the President of Tynwald. The ancient Sword of State sits in the chamber whenever the Court meets, usually on the third Tuesday of every month for up to three days, from October to June.

In the House of Keys, the lower Branch of Tynwald, sit 24 of those members. They represent not 24 constituencies but 15, as

Right & Opposite page: Twnwald Chambers

in the village of St John's is the Tynwald National Park and Arboretum. Home to tree species donated by countries from around the world, it was officially opened in 1979 by the President of Iceland.

GOVERNMENT BY CONSENSUS

Tynwald is the only parliament in the world which has three chambers – Tynwald Court, the House of Keys and the Legislative Council – and general elections take place every 5 years.

constituencies with the largest populations have up to three members. Originally the House consisted of the 'worthiest men' who attained their position through connection to worthy families or landowners on the Island. They meet every Tuesday except when the Tynwald Court meets or during recess, and are presided over by the Speaker.

The 11 members who complete the 35 are those of the Legislative Council, the upper Branch of Tynwald, whose main function is to revise legislation passed by the House of

Keys. Of those 11, eight are elected by the Keys to serve for five years, complemented by the Bishop, the Attorney General and the President of Tynwald. Originally the Lord's Council, it was made up of officers appointed by the Lord of Mann, each assigned a specific duty and who made themselves available for consultation with the Lord if he so wished. They also meet every Tuesday, with the same exceptions as the House of Keys, and are presided over by the President.

Unlike in the UK, government of the Isle of

The Council of Ministers

Government of the Isle of Man is based on a ministerial system. Following a general election, Tynwald Court appoints from its own membership the Chief Minister, who in turn selects those who will each head one of the government's nine departments. This body of 10, known as the Council of Ministers, is in effect the Isle of Man Cabinet.

Man does not lie in the hands of an elected political party, the majority of Tynwald's 35 members being independent.

The first Manx general election took place in April 1867.

THE ANCIENT SHEADINGS

For the purposes of census and local government administration the Isle of Man has three classes of district (town, village and parish) within the Island's six ancient sheadings (divisions) of Ayre, Garff and Michael in the north and Glenfaba, Middle and Rushen in the south.

The precise origin of the word sheading is not known but could be Norse, Celtic or Middle English. The Norse word skeid (ship assembly)

could imply that each sheading was duty bound to provide men to crew a warship. In Celtic gaelic it could relate to a word meaning sixth part, in which case it is feasible that the sheadings date from the 14th century under Scottish kingship. A third possibility is that it dates from the late 14th century, under English rule, when the word scheding meant administrative division.

Today the town districts are Castletown, Douglas (borough of), Peel and Ramsey. The village districts are Laxey, Onchan, Port Erin and Port St Mary. The parish districts are Andreas, Arbory, Ballaugh, Braddan, Bride, German, Jurby, Lezayre, Lonan, Malew, Marown, Maughold, Michael, Patrick, Rushen and Santon.

Above: The horned snuff box stands on the Speaker's desk in the House of Keys chamber

Opposite: Lots of three 'Legs of the Isle of Man'

6 | Business & Industry

A LESS TAXING WAY OF LIFE

Like the Channel Islands, the Isle of Man has long been known as something of a tax haven or, to use today's correct terminology, a low tax jurisdiction. Tax transparency around the world is continuously reviewed by the OECD (Organisation for Economic Co-operation & Development) which in 2013 awarded the Isle of Man the top 'Compliant' rating.

In 2013 the World Bank listed the Isle of Man within the top ten wealthiest nations, out of 214 international economies. This was in terms of Gross National Income (GNI) per head of population and lists the Island as eighth, ahead of the UK and the Channel Islands.

The island's residents and businesses enjoy the benefits of a taxation system which imposes no corporation, capital gains or inheritance tax, and a maximum 20% rate (compared with 50% in the UK) on personal income tax, much of which is taxed at just 10%. Residents also benefit from personal tax-free allowances.

In the increasingly diverse business sector,

Right: RBS International at the head of Victoria Street, Douglas

government grants are a practical incentive towards attracting new companies and a helping hand to those seeking to grow by investment, both measures having a positive impact on employment.

This relaxed overall approach to taxation is complemented by the Isle of Man's popular appeal as an agreeable and tranquil place in which to live, work or retire – summed up in the Manx saying 'traa-dy-liooar', meaning 'time enough'.

DOING THE BUSINESS

The Isle of Man economy has come a very long way since the days when the Treasury's coffers were largely dependent on the traditional industries of fishing, agriculture and tourism.

Measures put in place ahead of the new millennium and in the years since have achieved far greater diversity in how and where the island derives its income, creating a healthier and much more sustainable balance than at any time in the past. Isle of Man residents generally enjoy a comfortable standard of living and the percentage of unemployed is consistently very low. Towards the end of 2013 the unemployment rate on the Island was 2.3%, compared to 7.8% in the UK, according to the Office for National Statistics (ONS). Despite global financial troubles the Isle of Man's continued diversification looks set to

From left to right: Regent Street Post Office, Heritage Homes office, HSBC and Isle of Man Bank branches in Douglas

A slick business

Reports in 1957 that oil had been discovered on the Isle of Man turned out to be a hoax, but a controversial 1960s plan to build an oil refinery on the Ayres fuelled a major conservation battle. Strong representation was made by Manx residents after an American development company made plans to build at the Point of Ayre. It was a battle which protesters won, after a period of seven years.

Lady Isabella and Edwin Kneale

Robert Casement created Lady Isabella – but the Great Laxey Wheel's survival today is down to Laxey builder Edwin Kneale (1905–1993). In 1937 mine equipment was being scrapped and he leased the wheel, subsequently buying it outright and operating it as a tourist attraction.

In 1965 it was purchased by the Manx government and is now in the care of Manx National Heritage, which maintains the wheel in full working order following a systematic overhaul and conservation programme in preparation for the wheel's 150th anniversary in 2004.

keep the Island's economy within a steady level of growth, for over 30 years in succession.

The significant contributors to the economy today include information and communications technology, precision engineering and high-value low-volume manufacturing. The island's important financial sector imposes robust controls and is well respected across the international business community.

Shipping, professional services, film production, e-business and clean technology also figure high in Isle of Man enterprise and earnings. E-business, which includes e-gaming, is the fastest sector for growth on the Island, growing at around 10% per year. Recent

gaming events have attracted more interest in the Island as a potential base for software houses and gaming developers, while focus on skills development could further enhance the reputation of the Isle of Man into becoming a major hub for the gaming community.

AIMING FOR THE STARS

An example of a 21st-century science and technology business initiative which has really taken off is that centred on the island's growing aerospace industry. The Isle of Man Aerospace Cluster (IOMAC) represents a group of 22 companies whose expertise in advanced precision engineering is employed by clients such as Rolls-Royce, Airbus and BAE. Led by a private/public sector committee, and supplying both design and manufacture, IOMAC provides support ranging from one-off prototypes to full project management and delivery for a range of sectors. It is an example of how one cluster of businesses can group together and make their dreams a reality, and highlights the Isle of Man's 'can do' attitude.

In 2008 NASA's space probe *Phoenix Lander* detected traces of snow in the landscape of Mars with the aid of laser optics produced on the Isle of Man.

Another lucrative new opportunity is the growing market for satellites – not only in the manufacture of precision components but also for the incentive of the zero tax rate that the island's financial services sector applies to insuring launches.

As the sector continues to grow, so too does the need for highly skilled engineers. IOMAC now has a training programme in place for those wanting to work in this exciting area, and is something that will bring employment opportunities to the Island's youngsters who are aiming high.

In the wider context of space exploration, there are already far-sighted ambitions to create a pioneering new niche in the holiday market – the mind-boggling possibility of Isle of Man space tourism.

FORTUNES UNDERGROUND

Backtrack to the 18th century and potential

prosperity lay not in the sky but beneath the feet. There had been mining on the Island for centuries, with lead and iron mines first being mentioned in the 13th century, however the mines at Foxdale and Laxey started to exploit the Island's mineral seams, Foxdale in the early and Laxey in the late 1700s. Mining at Laxey began in the 1790s. Low pay in a hot and physically demanding environment, where accidents were frequent, led to miners setting up shops and welfare societies to protect their own interests.

By the middle of the 19th century increasing demand for lead meant that the Laxey mines' lowest depths had to be exploited, but flooding was a major problem. Ironically, the solution to pumping the water out lay in water-powered machinery. Although Victorian steam power was all the rage elsewhere, coal was a scarce resource on the Isle of Man.

Creator of the Great Laxey Wheel (named *Lady Isabella*) and architect of the mines complex was Manxman Robert Casement, a self-taught engineer. He also utilised water to power the other wheels, machines and turbines essential to the operation's success. At the time of the Great Wheel's opening ceremony in September 1854 Laxey glen employed 600 miners. For the rest of the century, aided by the Great Wheel, the mines

From left to right: Manx cheeses, Manx kippers, Flybe and EasyJet offer daily flights to the UK

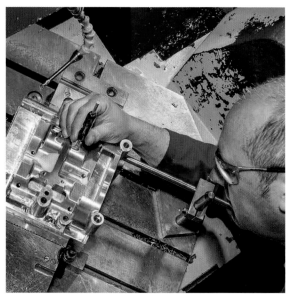

produced a great wealth of ore, peaking production in the 1870s. By 1929 reserves of the ore were virtually exhausted and closure was inevitable.

The history of Isle of Man mining has embraced the search for gold, uranium, oil, copper, lead, zinc, tin and coal.

THE ISLE OF MAN'S OTHER AIRPORT

Although still comparatively young as a flourishing industry, the business of making films on the Isle of Man is nothing new. In 1935 the motor racing comedy *No Limit* was released and proved a major hit with British audiences.

It was shot on the Island and its big star of the time, George Formby, was one of the most famous passengers to use the services of the short-lived but not forgotten Hall Caine Airport at Close Lake, near Ramsey.

Named after the Island's renowned novelist Sir Hall Caine, the airport served Liverpool, Glasgow, Belfast, Carlisle and Blackpool, where the beach served as a landing strip. Ronaldsway was then in private ownership. After a debate in early 1935 the Tynwald Aerodrome Committee decided that a government operated airport should be available to locals and visitors to complement the site at Ronaldsway. Located on land near to Close Lake Farm, situated on the road between Ramesy and St Judes, work commenced quickly and the airfield became operational under a restricted licence in April 1935, being formally opened on 3rd May that year. A full operational licence was granted in late July.

After expansion in early 1935, the airport reached its peak in 1936 with regular and frequent flights to and from the Island. Due to restructuring within the aviation industry, and with more traffic being diverted to Ronaldsway, flights to Hall Caine Airport dwindled in 1937. This led to scheduled flights to and from the airport being stopped, although private aircraft and occasional flights still kept the airport operational.

Requisitioned by the Royal Air Force after just four years' service, Hall Caine Airport closed to the public in 1939.

Salt of the earth

In 1891 it was thought that extending beneath the Irish Sea, towards the Isle of Man, lay a potentially lucrative coalfield. Drilling discovered instead a bed of salt covering five square miles and giving birth to Ramsey Salt Works, an enterprise which flourished. In 1902 the Manx Salt and Alkali Company Ltd was set up in order to extract the salt, mainly for industrial purposes. Laying a 6 ½ mile pipeline from the boreholes to a new panning plant, water was flushed down to the salt field and brine was brought back to the surface.

Eventually this type of extraction became uneconomical and the profit diminished, leading to the abandonment of the workings in 1956.

From left to right opposite page: Ronaldsway Aircraft Co., Swagelock, MEA and precision industry lead by the Isle of Man

7 Walks, Wildlife & Landscapes

WALKS ON THE WILD SIDE

The rail and tramways that cross the Island are survivors of the Isle of Man's golden age of tourism and as a total package are doubtless without rival anywhere in the world. Tourism still contributes to Isle of Man coffers and is focused mainly on special-interest holidays, events and activities.

Of the latter, walking's popularity endures and is yet another step back in time. The treasures revealed in the landscape include the breathtaking scenery, exposed cliffs and distorted rock formations found along the spectacular 95-mile coastal footpath, Raad ny Foillan (Road of the Gull). A variety of striking features bears witness to the fact that long before mankind invented weapons of mass destruction, geological evolution over a period of 490 million years has imposed violent upheaval on a scale to which only the forces of nature can aspire.

With a landscape little changed over the centuries, walking the Isle of Man allows you to enjoy the geology, flora and fauna over hills, moors, glens, wetlands and beaches – sometimes all in one day. While the Road of the Gull is a demanding walk, recommended only for the most experienced, sections can be taken at a more leisurely pace with no loss of enjoyment. And it's not the only walk to be had, from long-distance endurance to a quiet, leisurely stroll there are a myriad of walks to be enjoyed on the Island. Although the Isle of Man is small, no walker should be without a decent map, the Isle of Man's Public Rights of Way Map contains useful information on the many walks on the Island, and Ordnance Survey Landranger map 95 is well worth obtaining.

No visit to the Isle of Man would be complete without a trip to take in the Island's glens. Eighteen mountain and coastal National Glens mean you are never far from taking in the semi-natural delights of these preserved areas. Walk through woodland and lush vegetation, past streams, deep pools and spectacular waterfalls along the coast towards secluded beaches, or walk the mountain glens with their open moorland, tumbling streams and big skies.

Dhoon Glen is the steepest of the glens. Five miles south of Ramsey, the valley runs for over half a mile following a stream towards the shore, meandering along an old cart road through a dense canopy of trees. Here you will find the tallest waterfall on the Island, falling 130ft (40m) in two drops to the valley floor. No wonder photographers are attracted to this small part of the Island.

WILDLIFE SPECTACULAR

From the end of May to the beginning of July the Isle of Man puts on a rich annual display of wild orchids which is probably unrivalled anywhere in the British Isles.

Close Sartfield, a hay meadow nature reserve fringing the island's Ballaugh Curragh wetland in the north, shows off hundreds of thousands of flowering orchids easily viewed in their full glory from the reserve's trail. The second week of June is Orchid Week and guided tours add fascinating facts to fabulous flora.

Ballaugh Curragh is the first named wetland of international importance on the Isle of Man

Left: Maughold Head and lighthouse

Below: Killabrega

Next page: Sulby Glen

69

Above: Calf of Mann

Right: Wildlife Park

and has also been designated an Area of Special Scientific Interest (ASSI). Containing excellent examples of wetland habitats the area is also a breeding ground for the corncrake, one of the most highly endangered and secretive birds in the British Isles, and contains one of the largest winter roost sites of hen harriers in Western Europe.

Wild flowers, and particularly the 500 or so native species, play a crucial role in the conservation of much of the Isle of Man's wildlife. Around a third of these natives are in turn dependent on wetlands, the Island's most important habitat. Orchid species introduced number in the order of 1,000. In spring and summer these too paint a colourful picture in hills, meadows, verges and along the coast. Manx hedgerows are also an important area for the Island's flora and fauna. Without the use of pesticides the hedges, banks and sod hedges (a mixture of stone and earth) are home to numerous wild flowers that are rare outside of the Island, as well as being important habitats and wildlife corridors for butterflies, birds, lizards and small mammals.

In terms of geological time, the episode of rising temperatures, retreating ice and increased sea levels which separated the Isle of Man from the rest of the British Isles was a recent event, estimated at between 9,000 to

Left & right:
Basking Shark,
Risso Dolphin,
Golden Plover
and Hen Harrier

73

10,000 years ago. In the period since, the combined effects of climate, topography and human activity have influenced the nature of the landscape and the fauna and flora it supports. The variety of both wildlife and habitat is exceptional, enriched by the great diversity of birds and sea life attracted to the coastal and marine environments.

Habitat and species protection and conservation is the work of Manx Wildlife Trust, an independent charity, and around 3,000 acres of coastline and landscape are managed by Manx National Heritage. The island's statutory heritage agency, MNH was formerly known as Manx National Trust.

SAFE AND SOUND

By virtue of its name alone, the bird species most synonymous with the Isle of Man is the Manx shearwater – first systematically described by Francis Willoughby in his account of the 'Manks puffin' published in 1678. He made his study of the shearwater on the Calf of Man.

Since 1959 this small islet in the Sound, which lies on the migration route of many summer and winter birds, has been the base of a bird observatory for the work of recording and ringing, the latter being a harmless process. Wildlife conservation is focused not only on the Manx shearwater but

Left & right:
Common spotted orchid, butterfly and wildflowers in the north

Opposite page:
Point of Ayre

75

Missing mammals

For many mammal species common in Britain, the Irish Sea presented an impenetrable barrier to migration to the Isle of Man. Those notable for their absence from the island include fox, mole, badger, otter, squirrel, weasel and deer and, as in Ireland, there are no snakes.

On the other hand, enjoying the freedom of the Manx countryside today are two highly unlikely species – the red-necked wallaby and the European mountain goat. Both are descendants of escapees. The wallabies made a break from Curraghs Wildlife Park and the goats from a domestic herd.

Right: Spring at Patrick

Opposite page: Autumn fields in the north of the Island at Bride

also the chough, a rarity elsewhere but a success story here and present on the Calf all year round.

A less palatable aspect of the shearwater story is that in the past this ground-nesting species was regarded as a delicacy and a valuable source of income, and made easy pickings for locals and Isle of Man eateries.

Another traditional Manx breed which resides here is the Loaghtan sheep, used today to manage the grassland. A visit to the Calf can also be rewarded with early summer sightings of sea-life in the Sound – basking sharks, dolphins, porpoises or on rare

occasions a minke or orca whale. Nesting birds such as kittiwakes, shags and common guillemots, can also be spotted high on the cliffs.

The name Calf (Yn Cholloo in Manx) is derived from the Norse kalfr, meaning a small island in close proximity to a larger one. Managed by Manx National Heritage, and accessible by boat, the Calf of Man is a nature reserve of 616 acres, roughly 1.3 miles (2km) across. The observatory and information centre, based in what was previously the farmhouse, is manned from March to November by two wardens and has guest accommodation for up to eight people.

A WALK IN THE PARK

Orchids are by no means the only natural attraction of the Ballaugh Curragh wetland, the word 'curragh' in Manx meaning willow scrub habitat.

A nature trail runs through the area and information boards describe its complex ecology and the slow process by which woodland develops on open peat bogs. The trail also gives sightings of heron, geese and mallard. The observation tower offers the promise of further visual treats: raven, sparrowhawk or a songbird maybe. For some years the hen harrier made the Ballaugh Curragh a centre of international ornithological attention by virtue of its winter roosts, which consistently rated amongst Europe's largest, but more recently hen harrier numbers generally appear to be in decline.

There are no such problems for the popularity of Curraghs Wildlife Park. Its collection of animals and birds from around the world focuses on wetland species and presents them on a geographical basis. All grouped together with wildlife from the same country, you really can do a world tour in a day. Flamingos from Patagonia, lemurs from Madagascar, beavers from Europe, racoons from North America, Humboldt penguins from South America and wallabies from the Australian Outback are examples of the park's family attractions. A butterfly trail has also been built among the park's undeveloped

The Manx cat with a tale

Manx cats are known the world over for having no tails, and despite a reputation for being a difficult breed they have many admirers. One was no less an animal lover than Hollywood's Russian-born cartoon king Walt Disney.

In 1933 he received a furry new friend from the Lieutenant-Governor of the Island, on behalf of the people of the Isle of Man. Travelling from Liverpool to Hollywood via New York, aboard the transatlantic liner Franconia, no doubt in style, Manxie the pedigree black cat was destined to join the Disney studios. The cat was sent as congratulations for winning an Honorary Academy Award for the creation of Mickey Mouse and was presented to Disney by the English Consul in Los Angeles, Wentworth Martyn Gurney. Upon receipt Disney is said to have wired the Lieutenant-Governor: 'Cat arrived okay. A million thanks. Where is his tail?'

Whether this particular Manx moggy became the inspiration for any Disney animation antics is a question to ponder

natural areas to encourage the Island's native butterflies to feed and breed within their natural habitat.

Then there are hunters of the night – bats. In all, the Isle of Man has eight bat species. Pipistrelles, Natterer's and Daubenton's are among the species tempted to the site in search of unsuspecting insects.

DISCOVERIES OF GIANT PROPORTIONS

In 1819, when digging out his marl pit at Ballaugh, blacksmith Thomas Kewish along with brewer James Taubman, uncovered the skeleton of a great deer of Irish elk proportions. After being claimed by the Duke of Atholl, it was gifted to Edinburgh University Museum, and is now displayed in the National Museum of Scotland. Radio carbon dating techniques suggest that this specimen was in all probability the end of the line for the species – but not the end of the story. Philip Moore Callow Kermode, a noted Manx antiquarian who in 1922 became curator of the then newly-created Manx Museum, discovered a second giant deer skeleton in 1887, in virtually perfect condition, at St John's. This specimen was displayed in Rushen Castle until 1922 when it was moved to the Manx Museum, where it is still displayed.

Right: Manx cat

Sport

8

Despite the Isle of Man being a small Island, it is positively crammed with sports opportunities. Whether you love the thrill of a speedy motorcycle, the competitive edge of a yacht race or a gentle stroll along a golf course with world beating views, there is something here that is bound to get you outside and making more of our beautiful countryside.

MOTORSPORT

The annual TT races must be one of the best, and most exhilarating, free motorsport festivals in the world. There are no tickets to buy, just make sure you book accommodation in time and stake your claim to a choice spot overlooking the circuit. Many motorcycle enthusiasts return again and again, often to their favourite haunts, to witness man and machine in perfect harmony.

The Tourist Trophy motorcycle races began way back in 1907. From 1900 countries that had their own national automobile clubs had been racing motorcars in the Gordon Bennett Cup races, however with speed limits imposed in Britain the continental drivers fared much better. But in 1904 Tynwald passed the Road Closure Act, which allowed roads on the Island to be closed for road-racing, and in May of that year the eliminating trials for the Gordon Bennett Cup races took place. This was followed the next year by eliminating trials for the Auto Cycle Club International Cup event. In 1907 the Auto Cycle Club set up their own Tourist Trophy motorcycle races and the TT was born.

The 37.7 mile (61km) TT circuit, known as the Mountain Course, winds around the Island,

through towns and villages as well as through the countryside, and is world renowned for the skill needed to navigate the twists, turns and 220 corners. Motorcycling greats such as Joey Dunlop, Mike Hailwood, John Surtees, Steve Hislop and John McGuinness have all made their mark on TT history through the years. The current lap record is a staggering 131m/ph (211km/ph), quite a difference from the 40m/ph of the original winners of those first TT races.

Although the TT races are possibly the most famous events on the Isle of Man racing calendar they are really just the beginning of a great summer of motorsport held every year on the Island.

The Manx Classic Car Sprint and Hillclimb kicks off the year in April, where over three days competitors race for the fastest times in a mix of vintage, classic and modern cars. Then attention turns to modern rally cars in the Manx National Rally, before the Pre-TT Classics that highlight the start of the TT races. The Southern 200 in July features motorcycle racing on the 4.25-mile Billown road circuit near Castletown.

August is a month of motorsport with two weeks taken over by the Isle of Man Festival of Motorcycling. Run over the August Bank Holiday the Classic TT headlines the festival, with races and parades adding to the holiday atmosphere. The Manx Grand Prix allows amateur riders to live the dream and take part in four races over the TT Mountain Course, while the Manx National two-day trial closely follows. The Festival of Jurby involves motorcycles from all eras taking part in

parade laps and just as popular is the Manx International Classic Trial which rounds off the festival.

As summer ends the Island welcomes cars back to the calendar and Rally Isle of Man takes over. During three days in September rally cars compete on one of the most challenging courses in Europe as part of the British Rally Championship, over 160 miles of closed public roads.

Thanks to the foresight of those members of Tynwald who allowed road closures back in 1904 you're never far from world-class motor-racing of either the two or four-wheeled variety when you are on the Isle of Man.

WALKING

The Isle of Man was made for walking. You're never far from a good walk, whether it be a quiet stroll along a coast path or a vigorous mountain glen. But the Island is also the perfect place for those that like to be a bit more competitive in their walking. The 95-mile coast path 'Road of the Gull' (or Raad ny Foillan in Manx), was created during Heritage Year celebrations in 1986 and is a long-distance walk around the Island's coast that can be completed in a week by experienced walkers.

Once a year more competitive endurance walkers from all over the world descend on the Isle of Man to take part in the Parish Walk. Far from the gentle stroll it sounds, this 85-mile circuit sees competitors visiting markers in each of the Island's parishes within 24 hours. Definitely not one for the faint-hearted!

However, a much less strenuous festival takes place in the early summer. The Isle of Man Walking Festival, now celebrating its 10th anniversary, brings together walkers of all ages and experience to take advantage of the great outdoors. Guided walks occur all over the Island and are the perfect way to exercise while seeing the Island by foot.

CYCLING

With an abundance of trails criss-crossing the Island, and with a small population, the Isle of Man is just the place for cyclists. In fact the

Isle of Man produces world-class cyclists, as can be seen from Olympic and Commonwealth Games statistics. Mountain bikers are attracted to the rugged countryside, but it's just as good for those of us who prefer a more gentle time in the saddle.

Of course, if you are looking for competition the Island can provide that too. In September, mountain bikers from all over the world head to the Isle of Man for the End to End Race. Riding from one end of the country to the other, the route takes bikers along a 46 mile (75km) mixture of fast roads, moorlands, lanes and forestry tracks. Usually taking between three and six hours, the End to End allows for mixed abilities, making for a relaxing day out with fellow biking enthusiasts. The Longest Day, Longest Ride event isn't however for the faint-hearted – a 24-hour endurance mountain bike event held around the weekend of the Summer Solstice, where competitors ride for as long as possible around a 5km course.

GOLF

The Isle of Man is something of a golfer's paradise. With its mild climate and beautiful

Left: The TT races are depicted in one of the windows in St Ninan's church, Douglas

Opposite page: With the Isle of Man's northern plain in the background, Joey Dunlop leads Adrian Archibald and Ronnie Smith at Guthrie's Memorial in 1999 Junior 600cc race

scenery, visitors can play at all nine courses during their stay if they wish; indeed some people visit the Island just for a golfing holiday. With eight 18-hole courses and one 9-hole course, of varying difficulties, and with tuition and equipment hire available at many of the clubs, there really is no excuse not to try the sport.

The Island is home to the Castletown golf course, where golf has been played since 1892. Described as one of the best courses in the British Isles, Castletown was re-designed by course architect Philip Mackenzie Ross during the 1920s and 1930s, and has sea views to

with 26 affiliated football clubs throughout the Island, involved in all levels of the game, both male and female. The oldest club is Ramsey F.C. which was founded in 1885. The IOMFA is based in Douglas and runs the Isle of Man Football League, which is also known as Canada Life Premier League

Rugby is one of the oldest sports on the Island, with Douglas Rugby Union Football Club being founded in 1873. King William's College introduced rugby early in the game's history and a number of other schools went on to have their own teams. There are six teams currently playing Manx Rugby Football

enhance players' enjoyment of the game. Indeed it has been host to numerous golfing events over the years. Its 7th hole has something of an historic air, being the site of the first ever Manx Derby horse race, one of the oldest horse races ever recorded.

TEAM SPORTS

Being a small island hasn't proved to be a hindrance to the evolution of team sports on the Isle of Man.

The Isle of Man Football Association (IOMFA) has both junior and senior leagues,

Union – Castletown, Douglas, Ramsey, Southern Nomads, Vagabonds and the Western Vikings. They often play locally as well as in the English leagues, and there is also a National team made up of players from the six Manx RFU teams.

Cricket remains one of the Island's main summer sports. With history of the sport on the Island dating back to the 19th century, the Isle of Man Cricket Club (later named the IOM Cricket Association) was formed in 1930. Close proximity to the UK afforded the club a relationship with the Lancashire County

Cricket Board until the association was elected to the International Cricket Council in 2004. There are a number of clubs on the Island including - Castletown, Cronkbourne, Crosby, Finch Hill, Grasshoppers, Ramsey, Ronaldsway, St John's & Peel, Union Mills and the Valkyres. There are at present around 700 senior and junior cricket players on the Island.

Besides these three sports the Isle of Man also has a well established badminton association with both mixed as well as men's and women's leagues. The Manx Hockey Association oversees hockey on the Island, which can date games back to school and

anti-clockwise around the Island. The race sets off from Ramsey and is accompanied by a festival atmosphere for those watching progress from dry land.

Due to the varied conditions around the Island, from the sheltered east coast to the more turbulent north and south coasts, water sports are available for everyone, from the novice sailor to the extreme sports enthusiast. Kayaking has become a favourite in recent years, with a number of outdoor centres providing tuition for those wanting to learn the skill. There are also the more unusual types of sailing activities to be

Opposite page:
Extreme mountain biking

Left: *Enjoying the views from South Barrule*

college teams in the 19th century and the Manx Netball Association keeps the sport alive for a large number of clubs around the Island. Of course gymnastics and athletics are as popular as ever around the Isle of Man as they are elsewhere in the British Isles.

SAILING AND WATER SPORTS

Being an Island nation, the Isle of Man has a long tradition of sailing pursuits and water sports. Every year, in May, the Manx Sailing and Cruising Club organise the Round the Island Yacht Race where competitors race

celebrated during the summer months; for those with a more adventurous streak Peel holds the World Championship Viking Long Boat Races in June and Castletown hosts the World Tin Bath Championships in July.

EXTREME SPORTS

If you are one of the growing numbers of people interested in extreme sports, the Isle of Man can cater to your adventurous side. As well as having some prime rock-climbing areas around the coast there is an indoor wall in Douglas to allow dry climbing in a safe

environment. If you prefer tree climbing though, the latest adventure park on the Island is Ape Mann where old and young alike can swing through the trees on rope courses and climb trees up to 39 feet (12 metres) high.

There are also a number of outdoor adventure centres that have become established as places to either receive tuition or allow you to go your own way, whether it's kayaking, abseiling or wilderness training. One of the most popular new experiences is coasteering which combines rock-climbing with water activities in an extreme experience you won't forget.

ISLAND GAMES

Created in 1985 as part of the Isle of Man's Year of Sport celebrations, the Island Games (originally named the Inter-Island Games) brought together 15 small islands from all over the world for some friendly competition. Seven hundred young sportsmen and women gathered together to compete in seven sports, bridging the gap between local competition and the more serious Commonwealth Games participation.

The idea behind the Games was to compete

against other athletes who shared the same Island background, with the opportunities and setbacks associated with Island living. The inaugural games, despite being organised as a one-off celebration of sport, was such a success that it was decided to continue and to have an Island Games every two years, with Guernsey hosting in 1987.

The 'Friendly Games' was hosted once more on the Isle of Man in 2001 and has gone from strength to strength. More athletes are being attracted to participate and despite some of the Islands being more difficult to reach than others, competitor numbers have reached around 2,000 with 24 member islands taking part. Members range from the Falkland Islands in the south to Bermuda, Greenland, the Shetland Islands and Saaremaa in the east. The Island Games truly are an Isle of Man sporting legacy.

COMMONWEALTH GAMES & OLYMPICS

Manx athletes are some of the best in the world, as can be seen by their achievements in international competitions. Especially proficient are the world renowned cyclists and gunsmen that call the Isle of Man home.

Every year since 1958 the Isle of Man has been represented in the Commonwealth Games, and has won ten medals so far. Not bad when competing against much larger commonwealth countries. In that first year of competition Manx cyclist Stuart Slack won a bronze medal in the men's cycling 120 mile road race at Cardiff, followed in 1966 by Peter Buckley winning a gold medal in the same race. Two further bronze medals were won in 1970 and 1978 for women's swimming and men's prone rifle, then in 1986 Nigel Kelly won the Island's second gold medal for shooting. The 50m rifle prone men won the only silver medal in 1998, then in Melbourne in 2006 cycling hero Mark Cavendish took gold in the men's scratch race, while the clay pigeon trap netted another bronze. Two further bronze medals were won in 2010, for cycling and shooting.

Also important for the Island's sportsmen and women of the future are the Commonwealth Youth Games, which the Isle of Man staged in 2011.

But the Island just doesn't have Commonwealth medal winners, we have our own Olympic medallists too! While the Isle of Man competitors enter as part of the Great

Horseracing – the Derby

One of the earliest recorded horse races in history took place on Manx soil. In 1627 James Stanley, the 7th Earl Derby, staged the first Manx Derby on the Langness Peninsula, on what is now the 7th hole of the Castletown golf course. These races were meant to highlight the superiority of the Manx horse, a hardy but fleet footed breed, and a cup was presented to the winner. The 8th Earl continued the races, which were to take place on 28th July every year, being the birthday of the 7th Earl Derby. They were staged on the Island until the Derby was transferred to Epsom in 1779 and became the prestigious Epsom Derby of today.

Britain team... or rather Team GB, the excitement of a Manx medal is not diminished. In 2012 cyclist Peter Kennaugh won the Island's first gold medal in 100 years as part of the cycling pursuit team. The last gold medal was won in 1912 by Sidney Swann, part of the British men's eights rowing team.

9

Arts & Entertainment

ON THE AIR

Saturday 5th July 1930 was an important day for the Island. BBC Radio brought Tynwald to the attention of the world. After a programme by Miss Mary Kelly on Simple Village Pageants (one can only imagine now what that was like), 11am saw the Annual Tynwald ceremony of the Isle of Man being

Schools' Prize-giving by the Duchess of Atholl. Mr Morton had previously commentated from the Ceremony of the Keys at the Tower of London so was well known to listeners.

The Tynwald ceremony has been broadcast on the radio ever since, first by BBC Radio, then by Manx Radio and from 2009 has also been streamed around the world on the BBC website.

Right: Niarbyl was part of the backdrop for the film 'Waking Ned'

broadcast live to the UK. Starting off the coverage was a short explanation of the nature of the Court and its ceremony by the renowned journalist and travel writer H.V. Morton. The religious service was followed by the ceremony on Tynwald Hill, described for the audience by Morton, which in turn was followed by the

STARS OF THE SCREEN

What began in 1995 as an exercise in economic development has put the Isle of Man well and truly on the global movie map. The island's film industry is amongst the most active in the British Isles and in almost 20 non-stop years has co-financed and co-

produced more than 100 feature films and television dramas.

The attractions to those in the business of making films include the island's diverse landscape and choice of locations. To date the Isle of Man has posed very convincingly as Scotland, Ireland, Wales, England and even the Caribbean. The island's film-friendly government and population also play their part. To quote producer Martin Pope: 'Whereas in cities like London people see film crews as a hindrance, the island's locals are welcoming and friendly. Shooting a picture here is a real pleasure.'

Film making on the Island is nothing new. From the very beginnings of motion pictures, the Isle of Man has been an inspirational place for the world's cinematographers. As early as

1897 when *Diving at Port Skillion* showed images of men diving off a platform into the Island's open-air, men-only swimming pool, films have been making an impact. As the TT Motorcycle Races started their long ride into history films were being made to show the love of speed on the Island – in 1908 a film was made of the famous '4 inch' motorcar race, and of course, the TT itself has been filmed since it started.

Documentary makers visited to film the Island in the 1920s, while film-makers used the Island as a stage for more serious drama. The well-known Manx novelist, Hall Caine's works were adapted for motion pictures and filmed on the Island a number of times, all during the silent era, for example *The Bondsman* in 1928 and Hitchcock's *The Manxman* in 1929.

From left to right: Films on the Isle of Man: Island at War, Beatrix Potter and Relative Values

87

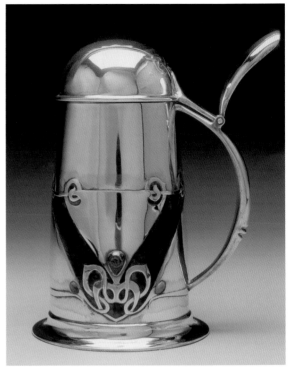

Above: Examples of the outstanding design work of Archibald Knox

Oppositte page top: Archibald Knox

Opposite page below: Maughold churchyard with the memorial to the novelist Sir TH Caine designed by Archibald Knox

The 1930s continued the film-making tradition and in 1935 George Formby visited the Isle of Man to star in the film *No Limit*, which used the TT Races of that year as a backdrop. For a celebrity such as Formby to arrive on the Island was big news, and as this became his most popular film the Isle of Man was put firmly on the map. Footage was used of the actual race, along with the crowds that went with it, bringing the Island and its racing tradition to a wider audience.

The 1940s onwards saw more documentary makers visit, but the film industry was moving towards Hollywood and the big British studios. The Island's films were seen more as a way of attracting tourism and showing off spectacular motor-racing than for drama. But as the years turned and rolling scenery and dramatic landscapes became more difficult to find unaltered, the Isle of Man again became a popular destination for the world's film industry.

When in 1995 the Isle of Man government realised the potential lying at its feet a structure was put in place to help the Island's film industry to grow once again. A Media Development Fund was put in place to help finance productions shooting on the Island, and despite ups and downs along the way, the Isle of Man has begun working with the Pinewood Shepperton Group. There are even film studios on the Island! With the diversity of scenery and architectural styles, the Island really can be accommodating for a wide range of productions. In 1998 the hugely popular *Waking Ned* was filmed on the Island as was the 2006 released blockbuster *Stormbreaker*, based on the novel by Anthony Horowitz. More recently, in 2012, the Island was used as the backdrop to a soon to be released period drama, *Belle*, based on the life of Dido Elizabeth Belle, the illegitimate daughter of a British Navy captain and an enslaved African woman, who was raised in England as an aristocratic lady in the late 1700s. Once again the Isle of Man is sure to be in the spotlight. With over 100 productions already under its belt, Isle of Man Film shows just what a special place the Island is.

Heritage with a history

Manx National Heritage originated in 1886 with an Act of Tynwald which established a body of Museum and Ancient Monuments Trustees. In 1951 this became the Manx Museum & National Trust. In 1991 a further change defined it as Manx National Heritage, the government's statutory heritage agency.

As custodian, its mission is to guard and preserve the Island's heritage for all, and to help the Island's population recognise their own unique culture and identity. Manx National Heritage is also at the forefront of promoting the Isle of Man to the world.

Nutty about Knox

One of the most avid collectors of the works of revered Isle of Man artist and designer Archibald Knox (1864–1933) is Hollywood star Brad Pitt.

When his son Knox Leon Jolie-Pitt was born in July 2008 a media frenzy began as to whether or not he was named after the Manx born artist. The Archibald Knox Society's website even included a welcome message for the baby, along with a picture of an enamelled silver cup and cover from the actor's collection of Knox's work. However, it is just possible that the child was named after his great-grandfather Hal Knox Hillhouse, we shall never know.

ARCHIBALD KNOX

When it comes to British Art Nouveau and the Arts and Crafts movements, Celtic design and establishments such as Liberty & Co, Archibald Knox is seen as one of the most influential artists of his day.

Born on the Isle of Man to Scottish parents, Knox used his home as design inspiration for some of the most iconic

Light and inspiration

For such a small island (618 acres/250 hectares), the Calf of Man has a rich lighthouse heritage – and surprising literary connections. The Scottish Stevenson family, leading lighthouse engineers of the 19th century, designed and built the Calf's early lights and that which stands on nearby Chicken Rock. A member of the same family was Robert Louis Stevenson, author of Treasure Island, which was first published as a book in 1883. Was he inspired by the Calf? And there's another story: in the late 1930s the Calf was purchased by a Mr Dickens – a distant relative of Charles Dickens – who subsequently donated it to the National Trust to prevent proposed tourism development.

An enduring story

The adventures of Thomas the tank engine and friends, set on the imaginary island of Sodor, may have been inspired by author Reverend W. Awdry's visits to the Isle of Man. With his brother George he worked out, in great detail, the fictional island's industry, geography, history and language, published in 1986 in a book entitled The Island of Sodor: Its People, History and Railways. It is highly likely that the name Sodor was derived from 'Sodorenses', Latin for 'southern islands', which by the 10th century were under the control of the rulers of Man and included Islay, Mull, Skye and the Hebrides.

metalwork of the early 20th century. His parents William Knox, a cabinet and machine-maker, and Ann Carmichael from Kilbirnie in Ayrshire, moved to the Island following the marriage of Ann's sister Margaret to a Manx fisherman, William Callister. Eight years after William Knox joined Moore's Tromode sailcloth works on the Island as a herring net machine maker,

on the 9th April 1864 at Cronkbourne village, his fifth child Archibald was born.

Educated first at St. Barnabas Elementary School and then at Douglas Grammar School, Archibald went on to study at the new Douglas School of Art and became lifelong friends with its headmaster Rev. Canon John Quine, both of whom shared interests in art and history. Throughout the 1890s, until his move to London in 1897, Knox continued his studies while earning a living as a teacher and had articles published on his research in leading magazines of the day, including the architectural journal *The Builder* and the leading arts magazine of the day, *The Studio*. It was also during the late 1890s that Knox began designing memorial stones for stonemason Thomas Quayle. Most of the memorials, around 36 in number, can be seen in New Braddan or Borough cemetery, both in Douglas and being designed from 1897 up until Knox's death in 1933, these can be seen as a chronology of Knox's style development throughout his career.

While teaching in London, Archibald became known to Liberty and Co, and by the turn of the century became one of the leading designers for the fashionable advocates of the Arts and Crafts movement. His 'Cymric' silver and 'Tudric' pewter are famous the world over as some of the finest examples of the British Art Nouveau style, and regularly attract high bidders at fine art auctions around the world. No one looking at examples of his mantle clocks of the early 1900s could dispute the fact that they bear no small resemblance to the Celtic cross slabs found all over the Island of his birth, and which he studied in great depth in the early years of the 1890s.

Knox spent the first two decades of the 20th century moving between London and the Isle of Man, with brief visits to America, before settling back down for good on the Island of his birth. By 1917 his association with Liberty was over and he concentrated on his teaching, drawing and painting watercolours until his death on 22nd February 1933.

10 Myths, Legend and Superstition

Being an Island with Celtic roots, and a history of Viking invasion, early Christian saints, Irish connections and Scottish and English occupation, the Isle of Man is as rich in folklore as any place can get. Very few of the stories and traditions of old were written down, the Islanders relying instead on an oral tradition to keep their heritage alive. As the Manx language started to die out, and visitors to the Island made their mark, English language writers started to collect the stories in order to preserve them for future generations. Authors such as British government commissioner George Waldron with his *Description of the Isle of Man*, first written in 1726 and A.W. Moore with his *Folklore of the Isle of Man*, published in 1891 did much to collect and save the stories and traditions that were quickly dying out. Today these books provide a fascinating history of the Island and make a fascinating read

SUPERSTITIONS

Being an island, the customs and superstitions of the Isle of Man have largely grown up around the sea. The population, being reliant on good weather and good harvests, over time built up ways of dealing with the fickle nature of the world, and like other areas grew their own ways of dealing with the harsh realities of a rural life.With many of the Manxmen occupied in fishing, a great many superstitions have built up around life on-board. It was thought that no fisherman should fish for the first time on a Friday as this would bring bad luck, and no fisherman would set out to sea on a Sunday either. No white stone would be taken to sea, and definitely not used as ballast. Whistling was not allowed on-board as it was thought to attract the merman or dooinney marrey, who in anger would take revenge by whipping up a foul wind around the sailors. Certain animals were also seen as harbingers of bad luck – hares, dogs, cats, horses and rats especially should never be mentioned. Even on land it was common to spell out the word R-A-T, or use the name 'long-tail'.

To counteract the bad luck that could befall a fisherman, Manx sailors had many forms of protection and ways to bring good luck. The cross-bone from a Bollan fish was taken on-board as a good luck charm, protecting against death and danger at sea and also thought to help steer the boats on course at night and when visibility was poor. A horseshoe was nailed somewhere on every boat, and on May-eve a crosh cuirn (or rowan cross) would be placed in each boat as protection. The wren was seen as a divine bird on the Island, to take the corpse of the 'king of birds' or its feathers to sea was thought to protect the fishermen from storms. If a storm did hit when the boats were out the fisherman's wife would throw salt into the fire at home to calm the winds, but if the wind was slack and not forthcoming a knife stuck into the mast was said to bring a more favourable breeze.

Superstitions however were not confined to the sea. Every home was filled with ways to make the most of the land and to protect farm and home from bad luck and the evil eye. Elder

trees were thought to be a protection from witchcraft so most cottages had one in their garden. Salt was a protection against fairies, placed around the threshold it would ward off the little folk and a small amount placed in any milk leaving the house was thought to prevent bad luck. This may stem from the fact that milk was a valuable commodity to the subsistence farmer and rural communities, and any waste or soured milk could mean the difference between a comfortable living and hunger. Fishermen also never let any of their salt leave their boat, nor even giving some of it to other sailors, as it was deemed unlucky. Superstition could also be linked to food. There was a superstition that a herring should not be turned on the plate, but eaten from one side, as to turn the fish was to risk the chance of overturning the boat from which it was caught.

The evil eye and witchcraft was also a dreaded part of Island life in days gone by. Hares were associated with witchcraft and were seen as a favourite form for witches to take. A hare that was actually a witch in disguise could only be killed by a silver bullet,

Getting into the spirit

On arriving at Ronaldsway Airport in 1979 to attend the Tynwald Millennium, the Queen was given a piece of silver fern to ward off evil spirits – an example of the many superstitions and tales rooted deep in Manx folklore. In times past, such beliefs were particularly prevalent amongst the fishing communities of Peel.

For example, it was bad luck to carry sea boots on your shoulder. After unloading a good catch and washing your boat down, if you didn't sprinkle it all over with salt you'd be inviting bad luck and evil spirits aboard. To guarantee a favourable wind it was best to tie magic knots in your handkerchief.

So real were these and many other fears that exploitation by those with few scruples was inevitable. There was money to be made as a 'good luck' doctor, prescribing preventative measures such as sprinkling boats with herb broth.

Left: Grammar School

and many an old woman was seen with injuries after a hare was shot by a Manx farmer. There were also many superstitions surrounding babies and childbirth. If a woman, after the birth of a child, did not recover quickly she was seen to be under the evil eye. In order to recover, a square of cloth was taken from the clothing of the neighbour expected of cursing her and burnt under the afflicted mother's nose. This was supposed to cure her of the evil put upon her. Newborns were also susceptible to the evil eye and in danger of being taken by fairies. Many preventative measures were put in place to prevent ill will, from keeping the child in the same room with food spread around the house for the fairy folk, to salt being placed in the mouth of newborns to ward off evil spirits and iron tongs placed over the cradle if a child was to be left alone. A child born with a caul, as in many other parts of the British Isles, was seen as lucky with the caul being prized by sailors as a charm against shipwrecks and drowning.

To help the population, as in most other areas of the British Isles, there were knowledgeable people, here known as charmers, who lived on the Island. Charmers were individuals who had the gift of being able to remove the evil eye and other afflictions. In a time before widespread healthcare these wise men and women healed and helped the Islanders with a mixture of herbs, folklore and common-sense. They would also help the fishermen to attract good catches and give herbs to alleviate periods of bad harvest and care for the animals.

TRADITIONS

As with the superstitions of the Isle of Man, there are far too many traditions to mention them all. The greatest and most important tradition on the Island is of course Tynwald Day. Harking back to the Island's very first government, this day, usually celebrated on the 5th July, is held at St John's on Tynwald Hill, which is said to have been built from sods of earth and stones from all of the Islands 17 ancient parishes. Here for more than 1,000 years the Island's government has met to pass

> ### Word of mouth
> *Apart from a Bible and a prayer book (both 18th century), and a Manx dictionary (19th century), very little of Manx Gaelic ever appeared in print. Tales of Manx myth, legend, folklore and superstition were passed on verbally from one generation to the next.*

laws, deal with disputes and see to the smooth running of this Island nation. Rushes are still strewn along the Processional Way in symbolic tribute to the Islands mythical creator, the sea god Manannan.

Another tradition that has lasted through the centuries is the Hunting of the Wren. Taking place each Boxing Day (or St. Stephen's day), the origins of this most unusual of traditions is lost in the depths of time, but may have influences dating back to the Viking invasions or the beginnings of Christianity on the Island, when pagan traditions slowly made way for the Christian festivals. Indeed the wren is the king of the birds to the Celtic tradition and is a symbolism of wisdom to the druids. In the early days of the hunting of the wren the bird was said to be hunted and stoned to death, however the event seems not to have been always attended to on Boxing Day, but may have taken place on Christmas Eve with the poor bird being used as a herald for Christmas Day itself.

Each hunt began with boys and men searching for the unfortunate bird, armed with long poles and moving from bush to bush, shouting and chasing with great revelry. When a wren was found she was killed without mercy and suspended in the centre of two hoops, with her legs crossed, garlanded with ribbons, flowers and ever-green foliage. A procession then followed from house to house in every village, while songs were sung. The feathers were seen as relics that offered protection and were offered to fishermen and villagers as charms to be purchased. By the day's end the body of the tiny bird was treated with reverence and buried in a corner of the churchyard, after which much merriment ensued.

Opposite page:
Onchan church tower

Whether the hunting took place to commemorate St. Stephen or to re-enact the catching of a seductress fairy who led the Island's men to their untimely deaths in the sea, this tradition is still upheld on the Isle of Man today – although for the sake of the wren population in these less bloodthirsty times the wren is replaced by a replica.

As with many areas of the British Isles, first-footing is a tradition on the Isle of Man, although here it is known as Quaaltagh. The first person to cross the threshold will bring either good or ill luck for the rest of the year, but on the Island the preference is for a dark-haired boy, and definitely not a female, a red-head or someone who is splay-footed... heaven help the person who sees someone who fulfils all three of these features!

Traditions on the Island tend to follow the Celtic year, and because of this there are many observances to take part in. Of particular interest, and linked to fairy-lore, is the custom on Mayday eve for the Islanders to make crosh cuirn, little crosses made from rowan or mountain ash. These are made without the intervention of man-made tools or iron, and so the twigs are stripped by hand and bound with hand-twisted sheep's wool. The crosses are then hung above doorways and cowsheds to ward off evil spirits for the year ahead. As you move around the Island you may spot some of these talismans still in use.

FOLKLORE

The Isle of Man is said to be protected by the sea god Manannan Mac Lir, from whom the Island is alleged to have claimed its name. Of Irish Celtic origin, Manannan means Son of the Sea, and his cloak of mist rises to shroud the Island from invaders in times of strife. But he isn't the only mythological entity to be associated with this lush, green Island, there are a host of fairies, elves and goblins who inhabit the Isle of Man.

Everyone who visits will know about the Manx fairies, however to stay on their good side it is wise to avoid their names and call them either the 'little folk' or 'Themselves'.

Opposite page:
Lonan Old church

Right: St
German's Peel

These are not the tiny, winged fairies that commonly grace the covers of fairytale books, these fey folk are around 3ft high, wear green or blue garments and red caps. They are also quick to take offence, so whenever you pass over the Fairy Bridge near Santon, on the road from Douglas to Castletown, be sure to say hello. Manx fairies are neither good nor bad, just like their human neighbours, but it's wise to stay in their favour. Many places around the Island have names connected with the little folk, such as Cronk ny Shee, which means 'Hill of the Fairies', near Malew, and The Fairy Hole, otherwise known as The Hall, which is a cave in the Sugarloaf, Rushen.

Amongst the helpful folk is the Phynnodderee or Fenodyree, a type of naked, hairy but helpful cousin of the fairies. This house elf was said to have been banished from the fairy kingdom for falling in love with a Manx maiden. Slightly clumsy, but a hard worker, this chap will help those he feels deserving, but never offer him a suit of new clothes – before you know it he will have taken offence and will have vanished into the ether.

The Glashtin can be a dangerous type. While in the water he is seen as a water-horse, and on land is more goblin-like, or seen as a real horse, however he is also known to take more human form, frequenting lonely spots and with a fondness for young ladies. Stories of the Glashtin show how, whether in horse form among the Islanders or as a more humanoid figure, he can drag unsuspecting people to their deaths in the sea.

The Buggane is an evil hobgoblin, so woe betide anyone who crosses him. It is said that St Trinian's Church was built in the 14th century on Greeba Hill, on the land belonging to the buggane, which infuriated him. Each time the church was nearing completion the buggane tore the roof off the building. By the time the third roof was being erected a local tailor named Timothy

Opposite page: St German's Peel

Above: Lag-ny-Keilley

Next page: St Michael's Chapel

99

wagered that he would stay in the church to finish sewing a pair of trousers. As he neared the end of his sewing the buggane towered over the church, but despite his anger the tailor completed his bet. As the last stitches were put in place the buggane was so angry he ripped off his own head and threw it at Timothy. Needless to say, the monster was never seen again, but to this day the church has remained roofless.

No place would be complete without a phantom black dog, and of course the Isle of Man has its own. The Moddey Dhoo is a black dog that is said to roam Peel Castle, and is one of the oldest known stories from the Island said to date back to the 1600s. At that time when the Castle was a garrison, the phantom would settle beside the fire in the guard-room and keep the soldiers company overnight, however he would arrive and leave via a passage that led from the Castle to the lodgings of the Captain of the guard. Over time the guards became used to the dog, but would always lock the castle gates in pairs, until one night a guardsman worse for drink decided to lock the gates on his own. At length he returned, full of fright, but would not divulge what he had seen. The unfortunate man died three days later and as a result the passageway was blocked up, and the Moddey Dhoo was never seen again..

Opposite page:
Port St Mary
cross

Above: *Eary*
Cushlin

11 Famous Children

Many remarkable people have either been born, or have spent their lives, on the Isle of Man. Let us introduce you to just a few who have called the Island home.

SAMANTHA BARKS

Born in Laxey in 1990, Samantha Barks is the Isle of Man's very own West End star.

Moving away from the Island at the age of 16 she studied at Arts Educational Schools (ArtsEd) in London. In 2007 she supported the Sugababes and Matt Willis at the Peel Bay Festival, and won first prize in the Maltese International Song Competition representing the Isle of Man.

Samantha's big break came when she appeared in the BBC talent show *I'd Do Anything* in 2008, in which Sir Andrew Lloyd Webber searched for a new, unknown talent to play Nancy in the revival of his musical *Oliver!* Despite being one of the youngest contestants she came a very popular third, behind second placed Jessie Buckley and eventual winner Jodie Prenger.

The West End, however, took note and Samantha went on to play the lead in *Cabaret* while also pursuing her music career. In 2010 she started a year long run as Eponine in *Les Misérables*, and was chosen by Cameron Mackintosh to reprise the role for the 25th Anniversary Concert of *Les Misérables* at the O2 Arena in London. She made her film debut in 2012, once again playing Eponine in the movie adaptation.

THE BEE GEES

Born in the Isle of Man to English parents, the Gibb brothers Barry, Robin and Maurice would later become one of the most famous pop groups of all time as the Bee Gees. The brothers grew up at 50 St Catherine's Drive in Douglas before moving to their father's home town in Manchester in the mid-1950s, where the brothers and their friends formed a skiffle band. The story goes that while performing to a record in the local cinema the record player broke prompting the brothers to sing live, kick-starting their singing career.

The family moved to Queensland, Australia in 1958 where the young Gibbs began performing. In 1967 after their first chart success in Australia the brothers returned to the UK, and with Robert Stigwood as their manager, *New York Mining Disaster* became their first international hit. The rest, as they say, is history.

WILIAM BLIGH AND FLETCHER CHRISTIAN

The mutiny on the *Bounty* has not just one but two Isle of Man connections.

Fletcher Christian was born on the 25th September 1764 just outside the Cumbrian town of Cockermouth. His were a branch of the Christian family from Milntown on the Isle of Man, an ancient family who's famous son William (Illian Dhone) was executed during the English Civil War. Fletcher Christian entered the Navy and in 1787 Captain Bligh appointed him as his First Mate on-board the

Opposite page:
TE Brown

Bounty, which was to sail to Tahiti to transport bread fruit to the West Indies. After more than five months on the island Fletcher led a mutiny to capture the ship and after seizing the *Bounty*, allowing some crewmen to leave, the ship was never seen again. Rumours abound as to the fate of the mutineers... some say they settled on Pitcairn Island where their descendants were found, with the group eventually being murdered by the islanders, however it is also said that Fletcher Christian returned to England.

William Bligh, the Captain of the *Bounty*, was Sailing Master on Captain Cook's ship the *Resolution*, accompanying him on his final, fatal voyage to the Pacific. Born in September 1754 in Cornwall, Bligh joined the Royal Navy at the age of seven, and went on to have an illustrious career at sea. Returning from Cook's voyage he married Elizabeth Betham, daughter of a Customs Collector from Douglas on the 4th February 1781. He went on to become the 4th Governor of New South Wales, Australia and rose to the rank of Vice-Admiral in the Royal Navy. He died on the 7th December 1817 in London, aged 63.

T.E. BROWN

Born on the 5th May 1830 to the Rev. Robert Brown and his wife Dorothy Thompson, Thomas Edward Brown is known as the Manx National Poet, and was voted the 'greatest Manxman of all time'. After the untimely death of his father in 1846, Thomas entered King William's College on the Island and went on to study at Christ Church, Oxford as a servitor. Although his time at Oxford was exceptional, Brown returned to the Isle of Man in 1855 to take up the position of Vice-Principal at his old college, King William's, and soon after married Amelia Stowell, his second cousin. He later moved to become headmaster of the Crypt School in Gloucester, before going on to teach at Clifton College, Bristol where he spent the rest of his working life.

His first Manx dialect poem *Betsy Lee* was written in 1870 and throughout that decade he wrote many more, attracting major publishers in the 1880s. Macmillan first published his famous Fo'c's'le Yarns in 1881.

He retired in 1892, by now a famed poet, and returning to the Isle of Man settled in Ramsey where he continued to write surrounded by his family. He died of a brain haemorrhage on the 29th October 1897 in Bristol, after returning to Clifton to visit friends.

MARK CAVENDISH

On 21st May 1985, the fastest man on two wheels was born in Douglas. His early years were spent riding BMX bikes, but by the end of 2005, the year Cavendish turned professional, he had won gold for Great Britain in the Madison track cycling event in Los Angeles with team-mate Rob Hayles. In 2006 he competed for the Isle of Man in the Melbourne Commonwealth Games, winning gold in the men's scratch race, he then went on to win gold again in the Madison, this time partnering Bradley Wiggins.

Cavendish is highly accomplished both on track and road, so much so that in 2011 he won first place in the world road race championships (the first British male champion in 46 years), the green jersey in the Tour de France and was awarded both Sports Personality of the Year and an MBE for services to British cycling.

JEREMY CLARKSON

British broadcaster and motor journalist Jeremy Clarkson is known for his unique, often controversial journalistic style. Writing columns for *The Sunday Times* and *The Sun*, along with hosting the BBC's *Top Gear* has made him a household name.

Born on the 11th of April 1960 in Doncaster, he lives with his family in Chipping Norton, but also owns Langness Lighthouse on the Isle of Man. His link to the Island however runs deeper than a holiday home, as his second wife Frances Cain is the daughter of Major Robert Henry Cain, a Manx recipient of the Victoria Cross.

DAVY KNOWLES

As Cultural Ambassador for the Isle of Man's Island of Culture 2014, Davy Knowles is

a home-grown talent who is forging a successful career in the music industry. Now based in Chicago, the singer, songwriter and blues guitarist, born in Port St Mary in 1987, made his US debut with his band Back Door Slam in 2007 before going on to concentrate on his solo career. During tours to support his first two albums, *Roll Away* with Back Door Slam and his first solo album *Coming Up For Air*, Knowles supported some of the biggest names in American rock, such as Kid Rock, Lynrd Skynrd. He was main support for Jeff Beck during his 2009 American Tour. Knowles' debut solo album went high in the coveted Billboard Blues Albums Charts in 2009, gaining number two position on two separate occasions, on the 11th July and 25th July.

Despite his huge work schedule Davy still manages to return home on a regular basis.

ARCHIBALD KNOX

Archibald Knox is a name synonymous with the British Art Nouveau and Arts and Crafts movements, his style being most famously seen on objects sold by Liberty & Co at the turn of the C20th. Born in the Isle of Man to Scottish parents, he was educated on the Island and became a student of the Douglas School of Art, where he would also later teach. In 1897 he left the Island to take up teaching positions at Redhill School of Art, and a few years later at Kingston-upon-Thames Art

Above:
Ploughing in the autumn near Peel

School. It was during this time he came to the attention of Liberty & Co. His Celtic styles are now recognised as some of the finest of the era, are highly collectable and regularly reach high prices at auction. When he returned to live permanently on the Island in 1913 he settled into a life of watercolour painting and teaching, and ended his collaboration with Liberty in 1917. He died in Douglas on 22nd February 1933.

NIGEL MANSELL

The most successful British Formula One racing driver, with a 15 year career, 31 grand prix wins and a World Championship under his belt, Nigel Mansell mixed determination with natural talent while on the track.

Born on the 8th August, 1953, at Upton-on-Severn, Worcestershire and growing up near Birmingham, he started his career young and became British Formula Ford champion in 1977. Surviving a number of horrendous crashes he went on to drive for Lotus making his Formula One debut in 1980 at the Austrian Grand Prix. He moved to the Williams team in 1985 beginning his winning streak, moved to Ferrari and then back to Williams, and in 1992 he took the World Championship crown but soon after retired from Formula One. After briefly driving in the CART IndyCar World Series he returned to F1 but retired for good shortly after.

Mansell lived in Port Erin during most of his F1 years until moving away in 1995. He was also special constable on the Island for 11 years while pursuing his driving career.

SOPHIA MORRISON

Amongst the famous Victorian sons of Man, Sophia Morrison shines as a daughter worth celebrating. Born in May 1859 to a respected merchant and ship owner from Peel, Sophia, the third of nine children, became well conversant in a variety of languages and became fluent in her Island's native tongue, despite her family being English speaking. She was a founding member of the Manx Language Society, and began a number of Manx classes, establishing those in the Isle of Man Fine Arts and Industrial Guild of which she became

honorary secretary.

Through her love for her heritage she became an advocate for Manx culture and became widely recognised as the leading authority on Manx folklore. A Celtic revivalist, her knowledge extended to both cultural and linguistic areas, encouraging a sense of national pride and preservation of the national Gaelic tongue. Her most successful publication, *Manx Fairytales*, was first published in 1911, however the second edition gained greater popularity thanks to the addition of beautiful illustrations by Archibald Knox.

Sophia died on the 14th January 1917 to much lament.

JOHN MILLER NICHOLSON

Considered to be the Isle of Man's greatest artist, John Miller Nicholson was born on the 29th January 1840 in Church Street, Douglas. The son of a painter and decorator, he followed his father into the family business, however it was his artistic painting that brought him widespread recognition.

A prolific artist, Nicholson sketched and painted the world around him in fine detail, aided by his sketchbook and later his camera. Rather than sweeping landscapes and posed subjects, he specialised in naturalistic scenes of everyday life from the bustle of the harbour to the tourists wandering around Douglas. The 1870s saw his paintings being exhibited at the Royal Academy in London, then in 1882, following advice from John Ruskin, Nicholson visited Venice after which his artistic style leaned more to the Impressionist style, capturing atmosphere and light on his canvas. Around the late 1880s he also illustrated A.W. Moore's *Manx Note Book*.

His art is highly sought after, with the Manx Museum holding a major collection of his work. Nicholson died in 1913.

HENRY BLOOM NOBLE

A Victorian philanthropist, banker and property developer, the name of Henry Bloom Noble can be seen all over the Isle of Man. Born in Clifton, Westmoreland in 1816 to tenant farmer John Noble and his wife Mary Bloom,

Opposite page:
Peel carnival

this businessman from a poor background rose to immense wealth and good fortune. Arriving on the Isle of Man in 1835, aged 19, Noble worked for Spittall's wine and spirit merchants, within five years he was managing the enterprise, and soon enough he set up on his own in opposition.

Moving into shipping in his 40s he was soon to become the wealthiest man on the Island. He was one of the founders of the Isle of Man Banking Company in 1865, in 1886 he financed Noble's Hospital in Douglas (now the

regularly performing at the Gaiety Theatre. Mollie lived in Port St Mary in the south of the Island for a number of years before returning to mainland Britain.

Born in Keighley, West Yorkshire on 21st July 1922, Isobel Mary Sugden studied at the Guildhall School of Drama following which she worked in repertory theatre and radio. She made her name through a number of television comedy roles, including Mrs Slocombe and Mrs Hutchinson, Sandra's mother in the *Liver Birds*. Married to fellow actor William Moore, who

Manx Museum) and in 1888 he saved the Isle of Man Steam Packet Company with a £20,000 loan. With investment in many of the Islands businesses and properties, his fortune was significant and on his death on the 2nd May 1903 his will saw him leave the bulk of his estate to charitable causes around the Island.

MOLLIE SUGDEN

The Isle of Man has also been home to a National Treasure. Mollie Sugden, most famously known for her portrayal of Mrs Slocombe in the 1970s British sitcom *Are You Being Served*, fell in love with the Island whilst

predeceased her by nine years, Mollie died on the 1st July 2009.

RICK WAKEMAN

Yes frontman, Prog Rock wizard and producer Rick Wakeman fell in love with the Isle of Man while visiting in 1987 and moved to the Island the next year. It was to be his home for the next 13 years.

Born on the 18th May 1949 in Middlesex, Rick studied at the Royal College of Music before leaving early to become a session musician, working for industry greats such as Elton John, Black Sabbath and David Bowie.

Joining Yes in 1971 thrust him into the limelight and he would spend the next decade working between the group and his solo work.

Moving to the Isle of Man allowed him to fulfil a lifelong dream of owning his own recording studio, where he produced two albums dedicated to the Island, *Heritage Suite* in 1993 and *Chronicles of Man* in 2001. He left in 2000 following divorce.

NORMAN WISDOM

One of the best loved personalities to

cinemas. His song *Don't Laugh At Me ('Cause I'm A Fool)*, first heard in the film *Trouble in Store* became his theme tune, however this 'fool' was a consummate professional. What was seen as spontaneous slapstick comedy was actually the result of much study and hard work; he was even Charlie Chaplin's 'favourite clown'.

Norman Wisdom had a charm and easy going manner that made him the people's favourite, and he was welcomed with open arms when he relocated to the Isle of Man in

Opposite page: Traditional ploughing at St Marks

Below: Viking festival at Peel

come to the Isle of Man must surely be Norman Wisdom. Born in Marylebone on 4th February 1915, Norman told how his harsh upbringing led him to join the armed forces where he became a bandsman and honed his craft as a fine entertainer and natural comedian. After seeing Wisdom perform in a Forces revue, the actor Rex Harrison persuaded him that he should take his chances as a professional actor.

During the 1950s and 1960s Norman Wisdom became a huge star, starring in 19 films as the hapless hero Norman Pitkin, his cry of 'Mr Grimsdale' echoing around the

1980 after falling in love with the Island during a season at the Gaiety Theatre in Douglas. He was knighted in 2000 and far from retiring he continued to work, only announcing his retirement in 2005 at the age of 90. He died after suffering a series of strokes on the 4th October 2010. As he was taken to his place of rest, the funeral cortege made its way along Douglas promenade where the Island's inhabitants gathered to pay their last respects. The whole Island was invited by Norman's family to attend the funeral service at St George's church, where Norman's life was celebrated

An Introduction to the Architecture of the Isle of Man

The Isle of Man contains many interesting buildings for the discerning resident or visitor to enjoy, with distinctive vernacular cottages, three castles (two built for defence, one built as a Ducal residence), works by historically significant architects such as M.H. Baillie Scott, Frank Matcham and Armitage Rigby, and other distinctive buildings produced through architectural competitions, especially in the Edwardian-to-Victorian era when many new buildings were commissioned. This book provides an introduction to this range of buildings stretching from the earliest surviving structures right up to the present. (Published by Lily Publications).

Churches of Mann

This case-bound book offers an overview of the history of the Island's religious sites. It features a wealth of colour photography of both external and internal views of the churches and chapels of the Isle of Man. Complemented by a CD of organ music. (Published by Lily Publications).

Saving the Gaiety

This book covers the restoration of this magnificent Matcham theatre. The title includes an account of the restoration of the theatre by Mervyn Stokes. 144 pages. Full Colour. (Published by Lily Publications).

Island of Barbed Wire

At the outbreak of war there were approximately 75,000 people of Germanic origin living in Britain, and Whitehall decided to set up Enemy Alien Tribunals. The Isle of Man was chosen as the one place sufficiently removed from areas of military importance, but by the end of the year the number of enemy aliens on the island had reached 14,000. With the use of diaries, broadsheets, newspapers and personal testimonies, the author shows how a traditional holiday isle was transformed into an internment camp. (Published by Robert Hale).

Manx Fairy Tales

This new edition of *Manx Fairy Tales* by Sophia Morrison has been re-edited into modern English for ease of read, especially for children. The book includes a CD with some of the tales being read by local Manx artists. The publication is also richly illustrated with colourful paintings by local artist Julia Ashby-Smyth. The book includes all 52 fairy tales over 112 pages. (Published by Lily Publications).

Manx Murders

Manx Murders is a gripping and mysterious collection of murder cases committed on the island over the last 150 years, from the brutal murder of a spinster one dark night on a lonely track near Ramsey to an equally savage attack on a widow in her garden in the busy centre of Douglas. (Published by Mainstream Publishing).

Profile of Isle of Man

New book covering the history of the Isle of Man written by Derek Winterbottom. 224 pages in full colour. A must to purchase to know more about the Island. (Published by Lily Publications).

Those Were The Days Volume I

This book brings together a selection of local archived images, which have been collated by local historian Richard Davis. The book incorporates a wide selection of historical pictures from around the island each captioned for the reader's interest. Volume II & III now available. (Published by Lily Publications).

Holiday Isle - The History of the Manx Boarding House

This colourful book overflows with life and fascinating old photographs of the Isle of Man's famous holiday industry. Stories are told from hoteliers, cooks, chamber maids and even the visitors themselves as they recall the heady days when hundreds of thousands of holiday-makers came to the Island for their annual break. (Published by Culture Vannin).

Wild Flowers of Mann

Authoritative and enlightening publication on the wild flowers of the Isle of Man. Superb colour photographs throughout with an easy-to-read approach and concise practical hints aimed at the readership for gardeners, countryside lovers, wild flower historians and residents of the Isle of Man. (Published by Lily Publications).

For full details of other Manx titles on the Isle of Man visit: www.lilypublications.co.uk